AGE of JAZZ
British Art Deco Ceramics

© National Museums Liverpool 2005

Published by The Bluecoat Press, Liverpool
in association with National Museums Liverpool
Book design by MARCH Graphic Design Studio, Liverpool
Printed by Compass Press

ISBN 1904438 27 X

AGE of JAZZ: British Art Deco Ceramics — Exhibition held at the Walker Art Gallery 11 June – 30 October 2005

Acknowledgements
Without the generosity and the co-operation of the lenders, this catalogue and exhibition would not
have been possible. I should therefore like to thank – Nick Jones, Michelle Forster Davies, John Clarke,
Audrey Barr, Lynne G. Cottrell, Lin Byrne, Lyn Ramsdale, Beverley, Nick Berthoud, B. Meyer, L. Adams,
Wayne Colquhoun, Muir Hewitt, Jill and Mike Newsham, Barry Davies, Paul Johnson, the Potteries
Museum and Art Gallery, Stoke-on-Trent, W. Moorcroft PLC, Burslem, Stoke-on-Trent, Manchester City
Galleries, The Trustees of the Wedgwood Museum, Barlaston and National Museums and Galleries of
Wales. I would like to thank the last three also for the photography of their ceramics.

My thanks also go to a number of professional colleagues for their help: David Flower, NML's Senior
Photographer, who was responsible for the majority of the excellent photographs, Lynne Edge, Head of
Ceramic Conservation who gave her advice, examined and conserved some of the ceramics. Senior
Designer, Simon Brooks, 3D Designer, Vivienne See, and Graphic Designer, Andrew Browne, for the
exhibition design. Robin Emmerson, Curator of Decorative Art, read the draft text and made many
helpful suggestions. David Moffat, Assistant Curator Decorative Art, gave practical help and assistance.

My very special thanks go to Rebecca Smith, my stalwart volunteer, for all her support and hard work.
I am grateful also to Colin Wilkinson and Michael March at The Bluecoat Press for their skilful editing and
design of the catalogue.

AGE of JAZZ
British Art Deco Ceramics

Sue Lunt, with contributions by
Paul Atterbury and Bevis Hillier

The Bluecoat Press

in association with

NATIONAL MUSEUMS **LIVERPOOL**

CONTENTS

INTRODUCTION

The aim of this catalogue and the accompanying exhibition, *Age of Jazz – British Art Deco Ceramics*, is to celebrate Art Deco ceramics made in Britain in the 1920s and '30s. Art Deco is the name given to the principal new style of the 1920s and 30s. The style came from France, and the Paris international exhibition of 1925 launched it on the world. Art Deco got its name only in the 1960s, from the words 'arts décoratifs' in the title of the exhibition. You can see the Art Deco style in the painting, architecture, film and photography of the period, as well as in the decorative arts. Art Deco brought together a wide range of influences and you can see this clearly in British ceramics. Many are stylish and well produced; some are cheap and cheerful, whilst others are plainly idiosyncratic. However, they all manage to capture the mood of the period with great vitality and often humour. Hundreds of factories in Britain were making interesting and innovative pots during this period. It is only possible to show a sample of what was being produced during what is known as the Age of Jazz.

ART DECO
THE INTERNATIONAL
BACKGROUND

by Paul Atterbury

At 11am on 11 November 1918 the First World War ended, after four years of conflict and millions of deaths, and peace returned to a world changed beyond recognition. Britain and France, though nominally victorious, had been devastated economically, and were facing the upheaval of social change. The British Empire, having carried much of the burden of war, was facing the challenge of independence. Russia, after centuries of Tsarist domination, was in the hands of the Bolsheviks. Germany, a new republic following the Kaiser's abdication, was facing famine, anarchy and Socialist revolution. The Austro-Hungarian Empire had collapsed, leaving the Balkans and Turkey in disarray and a power vacuum only partially filled by radical redrawing of the map of central Europe. The seeds of future conflict in the Middle East had been firmly planted by France and Britain. The United States, though a late arrival on the fields of battle, had tasted for the first time the seductive pleasures of playing on a global stage, President Wilson's fourteen points having been the basis of the armistice agreement.

At the same time, there was a widespread sense of optimism, underlined by relief that the fighting was over and hope for a future based on a new world order, and reflected by popular concepts such as 'the war to end war' and 'homes fit for heroes'. In many countries the spirit of the new beginning flourished amid the chaos and history was put firmly in its place – in the past. It was broadly accepted that in the new post-war world, political, social and economic change was both inevitable and mostly beneficial. The ripple effect of this process of change was all-encompassing, with new beginnings in fields as diverse as education and religion, music and sculpture and architecture and industrial design. These new beginnings were highly varied, but most took the form of a general pursuit of Modernism, on the basis that, as the old order had failed, the new order had to be better. Indeed, Modernism became a phenomenon of the 1920s, even though the way it was defined, and the way it was applied, varied greatly from country to country. These many contrasting and sometimes conflicting approaches to Modernism are the basis of the style now popularly known as Art Deco, a relatively recent generic term that has come to be widely, and freely, applied to anything designed or manufactured during the 1920s and 1930s. As a result, Art Deco appears to a modern audience to be a straightforward and easily defined style. The reality is very different – a series of widely varied styles reflecting diverse sources and degrees of nationalism, linked only by time and by a vague enthusiasm for Modernism.

In the aftermath of the war, France was a country beset by insecurities. Economic and political instability, racial problems, the lasting impact of the war, social divisions and a traditional approach to design and manufacture, all played a part. At the same time, France was the country that before the war had been in the forefront of Modernism: Art Nouveau, Cubism and abstract art, avant-garde music, fashion and engineering-based architecture had all made France, and Paris in particular, the centre of the modern world. By the 1920s much of this had been lost. The Paris Exhibition of 1925 was, therefore, a conscious attempt by France to put itself back in the Modernist vanguard and to rebuild in the process a sense of national pride. With this in mind, it is interesting to see, with hindsight, how relatively unadventurous the French displays actually were, with their emphasis on luxury and exotic materials, traditional forms and craftsmanship, and their reliance on decoration based on the stylisation of naturally-inspired and semi-abstracted forms. In many ways, it was the distant rather than the recent past that was the foundation for a new sense of national self-confidence, with the emphasis on the styles of the eighteenth and early nineteenth centuries. In effect, the basis for French Modernism was a Neo-Classicism blended with exoticism and decorative abstraction. At this time, style and decoration in France, and to a lesser extent in other European countries, were determined largely by the famous series of colourful pochoir-printed flat pattern portfolios by Seguy, Benedictus, Verneuil, Valmier and many others. These were used extensively as source material by designers and makers of ceramics and glass, woodwork, metalwork, textiles, tiles and wallpaper, jewellery and lacquer, as well as by typographers and graphic artists, illustrators, couturiers and interior decorators. As a result, there was a commonality of approach among French artists and designers in the 1920s which formed a strong and durable foundation for the development of European Modernism. This commonality also made Art Deco an accessible and easily recognized style, based as it was upon a limited range of much used motifs: animals, birds, flowers, fruit, sunbursts, fountains and fireworks, landscapes, exotic architectural forms such as the ziggurat, repeated geometric and abstract motifs and the delineation of speed. Such motifs were also universal in their appeal, underlining the genuinely international flavour of inter-war Modernism. In essence, objects or designs coming from France, the Netherlands, Czechoslovakia, Sweden, Italy and even Britain shared a common language, even though there were significant differences based on local cultural traditions, many of which reflected imperial colonial patterns. For example, French exoticism was drawn largely from West and North African sources, while in the Netherlands the Dutch East Indies was far more important. The British, as ever, drew upon a hotchpotch of colonial and trade-based sources that ranged from ancient Egypt to India and the Far East via the Middle East. In Scandinavia and in the new central European republics such as Czechoslovakia, folk traditions which underpinned a new spirit of nationalism were significant design sources.

Folk traditions and the exoticism of colonial inspiration were also linked by the cult of the primitive, another aspect of popular Modernism in the 1920s. Primitive was a fashionable word that could be applied equally to the use of African masks, Batik textiles, Egyptian ornaments, Norwegian folk weaves, Pre-Columbian gold and archaic Chinese jades or bronzes, as sources of form and decoration. The impact of primitivism was wide ranging and affected artists and designers as diverse as Picasso, le Corbusier, Lalique and Bernard Leach.

However, the French style of Modernism was by no means universal. In Germany and Austria things were very different, as they had been before the First World War when Jugendstil and the Secessionist movement had produced a far more avant-garde version of Art Nouveau based on geometry, abstraction and engineering. In the aftermath of the war Germany and Austria were determined to reinvent themselves in ways that removed any dependence upon the past. In both cases, long standing conservative empires were replaced by left wing republics committed to the establishment of a new social order. The past was consciously abandoned, and so new styles and new materials were de rigeur: industrial-style architecture, minimalist and functional decoration, concrete, steel and aluminium and an engineering aesthetic. The establishment of the Bauhaus at Dessau in the early 1920s was the tangible expression of all this, based as it was on the application of Modernist principles to all aspects of art and design education. The result was an easily defined kind of Modernism, universal in its application to architecture, furniture, glass, textiles or typography, that became, throughout the western world, the most direct expression of modern designs and modern living. Today, a chair by Breuer, or Mies van der Rohe, is a far more potent and universally accessible symbol of Art Deco than anything made in France at the same time. There is an irony in this, namely that Germany was one of the notable absentees from the Paris Exhibition of 1925, and was thus able to pursue a purer and more dedicated route to Modernism free from the all-embracing French approach to stylised decoration. In design terms, the First World War was still being fought.

The other notable absentee in 1926 was the United States. The Americans had appeared on the global stage for the first time in 1918, with a significant impact upon the last months of conflict. They had also played a major role in the lengthy Versailles peace conference. When those debates were finally resolved and the decisions applied, in ways that were to make inevitable the Second World War, the Americans withdrew from Europe, a withdrawal coincident with a period of isolation and introspection. In economic and political terms, the United States continued to dominate Europe, but emotionally the country turned in on itself, a reflection of culture increasingly self-reliant and detached from European concerns. Tradition was still important, but those traditions were now seen as American rather than European and so, in design terms, the United States laid the foundations for its own route to Modernism. This route was complex, incorporating elements as diverse as engineering and the industrial aesthetic, high rise architecture and the decorative use of modern materials and motifs taken from the native cultures of North and South America. The European design mainstream, dominant since the seventeenth century, was put aside.

Conversely, as the United States withdrew from Europe, its influence in Europe became steadily more powerful, thanks largely to two new cultural forms which had emerged in the aftermath of the war. The first of these was jazz, a new syncopated and improvised style of popular music with roots in ragtime, blues and other, predominantly black, sources. American jazz bands visited Britain and other parts of Europe increasingly from 1919 but far more important was the rapid spread of easily accessible recorded jazz and popular music. During the 1920s the combination of better recording techniques, initially acoustic, but electronic and vastly improved from about 1925, and the ready availability of the gramophone, opened up the world of popular music. Much of that music came from the United States, and so as jazz developed from its crude roots into the more sophisticated and smoother sound of the big band era, the impact of American culture increased year by year.

There were French, German, Danish, British and Japanese jazz and dance bands, some delightfully individual and eccentric, but they were all clones, shadows and echoes of the big American names. The proliferation of public radio from the early 1920s also helped to spread the message and the appeal of popular American music.

The second major American influence was the cinema, and in particular, the Hollywood fantasy machine that got into its stride in the early 1920s. Films made in America and starring famous American actors and actresses, exported American culture into every corner of the world. Most countries had their own film industry, but few of these could ever compete with American cinema in terms of universal appeal. The dominance of American films increased steadily through the period, reflective as they were, more and more, of contemporary American life and American cultural attitudes. As a result, American Modernism became universally accessible and familiar through the medium of the cinema. Relatively few people actually travelled to the United States, but they did not need to, for a visit to the local Odeon on a Saturday night would give them the complete American experience. Indeed, one of the best ways even today to grasp the American vision of Modernism is to watch a 1930s musical such as 42nd Street, Flying Down to Rio, or Swingtime.

American attitudes to Europe, and indeed to itself, were shifted seismically by the Wall Street Crash of 1929, and the ripple effect of this financial cataclysm reached every corner of the world. American isolation and introspection became more intense, but perversely Europe became even more dependent upon the United States, culturally and financially. And every cinema and every record store offered a direct route to the heart of modern America.

The result was, inevitably, a major shift in design terms away from Europe and towards the United States. The influence of France and French style diminished, as did the jazz, colourful and eccentric Modernism so popular in the 1920s. Stylised nature, angular forms and decorative abstraction, of the kind epitomised in Britain by Clarice Cliff, yielded to soft, rounded forms, pastel colours, matt finishes and a greater dependence upon architecture and engineering. The German Bauhaus designers, more in tune with this approach, had in any case moved to the United States by the early 1930s, having been driven out of Europe by the rise of fascism, a move that underlined the cultural closeness between the two countries.

Industrial design, in the true modern meaning of the term, emerged in the United States in the 1930s, in the work of luminaries such as Teague, Desky and Loewy, men who through their writings and their work for the consumer market, gave design a status that it had probably never enjoyed before.

American style and American design, familiar globally through films, exhibitions, books and magazines, dominated the 1930s and, in effect, launched the second phase popular Modernism, or Art Deco. This was characterised by a cool elegance, a sense of modernity derived from the machine ethic and a formalised functionalism that was at the same time decorative – an approach to design typified by the ocean liner, the long distance train, the luxury automobile and, to a lesser extent, the aeroplane. The Art Deco era was, without doubt, the great age of travel, and ships, trains and planes were getting better, going faster and looking more stylish year by year. They also represented international Modernism in a very accessible way. As a result, there was a direct influence upon architecture, interior design and the consumer market, with objects as diverse as teapots, pencil sharpeners and toasters beginning to look like parts of ships or aeroplanes. Domestic architecture began to look like a blend between an ocean liner and a factory and there was, at the same time, a vogue for films with futuristic themes. The most direct effect of all this was a passion for streamlining, to be seen through the 1930s in the design for all kinds of domestic and consumer objects, in typography, graphics and advertising, in fashion and even in the decorative bronzes of Chiparus and the carvings of Henry Moore. Streamlining, clearly useless in all these areas, and actually only of limited use for ships and trains, was the decorative fantasy that determined the nature of design in the 1930s, and became the characterising element of the contemporary vision of Art Deco.

PAUL ATTERBURY Lecturer, writer, broadcaster, exhibition curator, specialising in art and design of the 19th and 20th centuries. Formerly editor of the Connoisseur. Curator of exhibitions at the Victoria & Albert Museum, including Pugin (1994) and the Victorian Vision (2001).

He has written over 30 books, on ceramics, art and design, railways and canals. For 15 years he has been a member of the BBC's *Antiques Roadshow* team of experts.

THE PLACE OF BRITISH ART DECO CERAMICS

by Bevis Hillier

In 2004 the Brazilian-born footballer Anderson Luis de Souza Deco was much in the news. It was generally agreed that the 25-year-old player was the star of his team, Porto, which became champions of the Portuguese League in 2003-4. On the sports pages, British newspaper sub-editors gave the accounts of his exploits such headlines as 'ARTFUL DECO' and 'THE ART OF DECO'. Those headlines showed that the term Art Deco had so far penetrated demotic English language that even football fans – not all noted as passionate aesthetes – could be expected to pick up the punning allusions. Yet 'Art Deco' – a term covering the design and decorative arts of the 1920s and 30s – was a comparative newcomer to the language and had only recently been received into the *Oxford English Dictionary*. During the 1920-40 period itself, the style (really a congeries of styles) was known as 'Jazz Modern' or '*moderne*'.

In 2003 the Victoria & Albert Museum in London held a major exhibition of Art Deco. Reviewing it in *The Sunday Times*, the paper's art critic, Waldemar Januszczak, wrote:

> I was astonished to find that Art Deco has only been called Art Deco since about 1970. Does everyone else know this? Am I the only sucker in the antique shop who assumed it to be an elegant, historic *nom d'esprit* created by Parisian style makers in about, oh I don't know … 1927? It appears that a book describing and defining the girl-and-greyhound look came out in 1968, and after that it took no time to catch on. For half a century it did not have a proper brand name. Suddenly there was one.

> All this is remarkable not only for the many decades that were needed to find a label that stuck to the glass. Just as intriguing, surely, is the immediate success of the new name once it began circulating. It must have spread as fiercely as a cow disease. I can vividly remember going into junk shops in Manchester in the early 1970s and bandying the tag about merrily as I laid out for my very own girl and greyhound. I presume I picked it up from the junk dealers. The must have learnt it from the book. Powerful junk-shop forces would have been at work here. Tons of stuff needed shifting. A catchy cultural tag was needed to shift it. Three decades before the triumph of Nike, we were witnessing the transformative power of successful branding. A tsunami of frustrated desire must have surged through the jumble sales, junk shops and bring-and-buy occasions as Hurricane Deco hit the recycling market.

I wrote the book that Januszczak refers to. Entitled *Art Deco of the 20s and 30s*, it was published in London in 1968 and in New York in 1969. As he suggests, it is credited with popularizing the term Art Deco internationally. (It beat off a rearguard action that favoured 'streamline *moderne*'.) But I did not invent the term. As I was careful to point out in the book, the phrase was already in limited use, by some collectors and journalists, in 1966. I first heard it from the dealer John Jesse who, then as now, was selling Art Nouveau and Art Deco in his shop in Kensington Church Street, London. With a muffled giggle, he said: 'Do you know they're calling that stuff? *Art Deco!*' I was already planning a book on the decorative arts of the between-two-wars period, and I realised this would be the perfect title for it. The term 'Art Deco' was derived from a Paris exhibition of 1925 – the *Exposition Internationale des Arts Décoratifs et Industriels* – in which the new style was first seen, *en masse*, in its fully developed form. Pioneers are bound to make mistakes, get some emphases wrong and I must admit there was one glaring gap in my little book of 1968, with its orange, green and black cover. I had never been to the United States, and there was virtually nothing in the book about skyscrapers and other expressions of American Deco. (That was remedied in 1971 when I organised a big exhibition of Art Deco in Minneapolis.) But the 'working definition' of Art Deco which I suggested near the beginning of the book still, I think, holds good today:

> An assertively modern style, developing in the 1920s and reaching its high point in the '30s; it drew inspiration from various sources, including the more austere side of Art Nouveau, Cubism, the Russian Ballet, American Indian art and the Bauhaus; it was a classical style in that, like Neo-Classicism but unlike Rococo or Art Nouveau, it ran to symmetry rather than asymmetry, and to the rectilinear rather than the curvilinear; it responded to the demands of the machine and of new materials such as plastics, ferro-concrete and vita-glass; and its ultimate aim was to end the old conflict between art and industry, the old snobbish distinction between artist and artisan, partly by making artists adept at crafts, but still more by adapting design to the requirements of mass-production.

In the same book I wrote that Art Deco was 'the last of the total styles'. I think that still holds good, too. A case might be made for the 1950s style known in that decade as 'Contemp'ry', with its boomerang shapes and bobble legs, but it did not affect *everything,* as Art Deco did – hotels, liners, letterboxes, handbag-clasps and teapots.

Art Deco was a promiscuously eclectic style; but, fundamentally, it might be described as 'domesticated cubism'. It found a way of absorbing the revolutionary innovations of Picasso and Braque into the bloodstream of design – in linoleum, wallpaper, textiles, furniture, silver … and ceramics. The preceding style of Art Nouveau, which flourished (roughly speaking) from 1890 to the end of the First World War, had already been moving in the direction of the hard-edge and rectilinear, notably with the architecture and furniture of Charles Rennie Mackintosh and Josef Hoffmann's Palais Stoclet, Brussels (1906-11). The Michelin Building in London (1911-12), with its panels of coloured tiles representing automobiles, is a classic example of the transition between late Art Nouveau and Art Deco. So is Royd House, Hale, Manchester (1914-16), with its bold zigzag façade patterns, a building designed by Edgar Wood for his own use.

Art Deco drew on many other influences besides that of fag-end Nouveau. The Russian Ballet gave it vivid, exotic colours. (The Russian-born Deco artist Erté was a disciple, at one remove, of Léon Bakst.) American Indian art also had a big effect, especially in the stepped shape of Mayan temples. The sensational opening of Tutankhamun's tomb in 1922 brought scarabs, sphinxes and pyramids into the decorative arts. And world history must not be disregarded as an influence. At the end of the First World War, a need was felt for some fizz and frivolity after the five mournful years that had just passed. People sought an art that was cheering. In the thirties, by contrast, with hunger marches in England and the rise of Nazism in Germany, life became more serious and political. The writer and Vorticist artist Wyndham Lewis (who became Fascist and wrote an early eulogy of Hitler in 1930) welcomed this change. 'The world was getting, frankly, extremely silly,' he wrote. '… There must obviously arrive a point at which a breath of sense would break into it suddenly, and blow it all over.' The cartoonist Osbert Lancaster, whose antennae always quivered at the slightest nuance of social or cultural change, was much less enthusiastic. He observed 'some profound and, to me, depressing changes' in the Oxford which followed his time (the late 1920s) as an undergraduate:

> Aesthetics were out and politics were in, and sensibility was replaced by social awareness. Figures such as [Richard] Crossman, 'broad of Church and broad of mind, broad before and broad behind', who as undergraduates had been widely regarded as jokes, as young dons now loomed large with prophetic menace. In Blackwell's the rainbow hues of the Duckworth collected Firbank were soon overwhelmed by the yellow flood of the Left Book Club, and the recorded strains of 'Happy days are here again' floating across the summer quad were drowned by the melancholy cadences of 'Hyfrydwl' chanted live by Welsh miners trekking southwards down the High. Martinis and champagne had given way to sherry and beer; serious-minded, aggressive pipes had ousted the gold-tipped Balkan Sobranie of yesteryear; Sulka shirts and Charvet ties were now outmoded by thick dark flannel and hairy tweed.

The social changes were reflected in Art Deco. Just as Art Nouveau had been transmuted from the curvilinear style of the 1890s to the rectilinear of the early 1900s, so Art Deco of the 1920s – which might most typically be represented by stylized flowers cascading out of a fancy basket – morphed in the thirties into something more uncompromisingly geometric, less pretty-pretty.

In some ways, pottery and porcelain were not the perfect vehicles for such a style. In the same year that my first Art Deco book was published – 1968 – I also published a book on *Pottery and Porcelain 1700-1914*. In a chapter on 'The end of the Baroque' I wrote:

> In the baroque period, all the arts aspired towards the condition of grand opera. The richest fulfilment of the style was in palace and castle architecture, heroic tragedy, opera, oratorio and fantastic masques, which, by requiring an imposing congress of art forms, gave scope for the talents of an *uomo universale* such as Bernini. Such a style was not ideally suited to ceramics. Porcelain was too frail, pottery too homely, for its hyperboles and ecstasies; and ceramics cracked in the kiln if used on too grand a scale.

How different (I suggested in a later chapter) was the case of the Rococo style, whose asymmetry and shell-like whorls and curlicues lent themselves to infinitely malleable clay. That malleable quality of clay – a need to knead, as it were – is pretty redundant in Art Deco ceramics. While one must admit that the natural outcome of clay on the potter's wheel or the turner's lathe is symmetry, with many Deco ceramics there is a feeling that the creative artist is working, so to speak, against the grain, dragooning the clay into angles, including right angles, for which it is not the natural medium. Some might disagree with that view; but, if anything, the consciousness that the Deco potter is, in a sense, at war with his or her material, should increase, rather than detract from, our admiration for the resulting triumphs.

Whether or not to adopt the Art Deco style was, for British potters, less an aesthetic decision than a marketing one. Would people buy it? Most of the potters were inclined to be cautious, were slow to 'convert'. Some never converted at all. The technically exquisite Carlton ware is only rarely whole-hoggingly Deco. Much of the decoration is of leaves and tendrils: here there is more in common with Art Nouveau, which turned to motifs from nature and away from 'historicism' such as Renaissance lambrequins. The fey scenes depicted in Carlton's 'Moonlight Cameo' pattern (no. 2944) belong more with the fairyland idylls of the early 1900s, *Peter Pan* (1904) and the poetry of Madison Cawein and Walter de la Mare, than with the fragmented, speeded-up world of the inter-war years; and the panels in which they were set appeared on fairly traditional shapes. The 'Fairyland Lustre' designed for Wedgwood by Daisy Makeig-Jones – with breathtaking skill – is of the same elfin genre. Charlotte Rhead was working throughout the Deco period and was still making pots in 1942, five years before her death; but she rarely paid much more than lip service to the Deco style. On Poole pottery is often found the leaping gazelle motif, perhaps only rivalled by the sunray as a key ingredient of Deco design; yet the wares generally have more in common with rural folk art – say, that of Czechoslovakia or Hungary – than with the jazzy, modernistic, metropolitan Deco style. They did however, make some pieces that were as good as the French could produce. The Dedham and Maling Potteries were both inclined to conservatism in their wares. One factory that one might have expected to be reactionary was Burleigh of Burslem. It was founded in 1862 as Burgess & Leigh Ltd., and five generations of the Leigh family were sole owners of the pottery from 1912 until 1999. (The Grade II-listed bottle oven and factory have been preserved.) Yet in fact Burleigh made flamboyantly Deco wares, such as the 'Carnival' range of 1929, and novelties like the 1932 'Guardsman' jug in the form of marching soldiers. Julie McKeown, who in 2004 published an admirable book on the factory, thinks that the Leighs were influenced by the wares of Clarice Cliff.

Cliff is of course the artist who finds Deco most congenial. She is not only the queen of ceramic deco; at their best, her designs deserve to be considered as part of mainstream Cubism, not just offshoots from it (though perhaps she was a little optimistic in naming one of her patterns 'Mondrian'). To make a slightly less high-falutin claim, she brought to ceramics something very similar to Walt Disney's simplified fantasy: her 'Bizarre' range was introduced in 1928, the year of Mickey Mouse's debut in New York. As with Disney, her work is often humorous; and that is an attribute which distinguishes British ceramic designers in general from those on the Continent. (Think of Louis Wain's ceramic cats!) If we look at French ceramics of the period – by such as René Buthaud, Emile Lenoble, Sèvres, Boch Frères and Jean Mayodon – we find a high-minded and ambitious striving (often beautifully achieved) for 'purity of form', refinement and tastefulness, but the element of comedy is absent.

Susie Cooper is another great potter who takes to Deco, particularly in her 'banded' wares: this is a chameleon-like genius who, some 20 years later, shows an equal facility for making the 1950s 'Contemp'ry' style her own. Shelley, in their tea-sets in the so-called 'Eve' shape, and Midwinter, in wares so Cubistic as to be verging on comical impracticality, also surrendered to the Deco movement: older customers might have thought a Shelley service too new-fangled and jazzy, but a young couple might welcome it as a wedding-present. Keith Murray and John Skeaping designed wares of stepped Deco shape – inverted ziggurats – for Wedgwood. Doulton, in Stoke, made figurines which were the ceramic equivalent of the chryselephantine figures of bronze and ivory by Demètre Chiparus and Ferdinand Preiss: technically impeccable, slightly naughty and rather kitsch. (Paul Johnson, who grew up in the Staffordshire Potteries, remembers a Doulton figure designed by Leslie Harradine. 'The Harradine figure which fascinated me … was 'The Bather', always displayed at home, high up on the shelves, with her brilliant blue-and-purple wrap showing. But if you turned her round she was naked and was known to the family as 'The Rude Lady'.)

That women like Cliff and Cooper were among the leading figures in Art Deco ceramics – is no surprise. The First World War siphoned off men from the factories, leaving a vacuum (Cliff joined Wilkinson's in 1916); and many of the men never returned. But in any case, women had been employed in large numbers in the Potteries for years. In *Anna of the Five Towns* (1902), Arnold Bennett described the painting shop at a potbank.

> The paintresses form the noblesse of the banks [ie potbanks]. Their task is a light one, demanding deftness first of all; they have delicate fingers, and enjoy a general reputation for beauty; the wages they earn may be estimated from their finery on Sundays. They come to business in cloth jackets, carry dinner in little satchels; in the shop they wear white aprons, and look startlingly neat and tidy.

Clarice Cliff began work as an apprentice enameller at Lingard Webster and Company only ten years after those words were written. She was 13 then. Her childhood was spent in the Potteries scene evoked in Bennett's novels. His description of a school treat picnic sounds just like a Cliff design, even down to the gaudy colours with which he invests the landscape.

> The sun shone generously on scores of vivid and frail toilettes, and parasols made slowly-moving hemispheres of glowing colour against the rich green of the grass. All around were yellow cornfields, and meadows where cows of a burnished brown indolently meditated upon the phenomena of a school-treat. Every hedge and ditch and

gate and stile was in that ideal condition of plenary correctness … The sky, of an
intense blue, was a sea in which large white clouds sailed gently but capriciously …

In 1964 I travelled to Stoke-on-Trent to do some research for my first book, *Master Potters of
the Industrial Revolution: The Turners of Lane End* (1965). Living then in London, with its endless
suburbs, the first thing that struck me, on the train journey, was the startling way country very
abruptly gave way to town, green fields to sooty factories and houses. In the Five Towns they still
sold black-and-white postcards showing bottle ovens streaming black smoke. The cards had jokey
captions – 'The air soots me well' and 'Shadows of the evening steal across the sky' (the latter,
from Sabine-Gould's hymn 'Now the day is over'). But the bottle ovens were fast vanishing. On
my visit I met Reginald Haggar, the Potteries historian and artist, who had been seen to weep
when an eighteenth-century oven was demolished. My visit of 1964 was much nearer the Art
Deco period than the present is near 1964. I remember women pottery workers in clogs,
walking hand-in-hand – a custom that would have been taken as Sapphic in London then.
   When we enjoy the springtime freshness and vivacity of Clarice Cliff's wares, or Susie
Cooper's, we ought to remember the Stygian industrial setting in which they were created. For a
masterly evocation of that scene, we can turn to *The Vanished Landscape: A 1930s Childhood in
the Potteries* (2204) by Paul Johnson, the former editor of the *New Statesman*.

> I can see the tall chimneys, belching smoke [he writes], the distant winding
> towers of the coal pits, above all the bottle-shaped pot-banks, each individual,
> each slightly different, clustered in families, around their courtyards.

Johnson's mother, a Manchester woman, was 'horrified' by the Potteries. 'Partly by its poverty, for
it was a low wage area, as were all industries in those days which employed a high percentage of
women and girls'. Mrs Johnson complained, 'They burn disgusting cheap slack instead of real
Wigan coal, and you can hear it exploding in the ovens and see it jumping up the pot-banks in
great showers of sparks … A beautifully washed man's shirt comes back in the evening battle-
ship grey, or *worse*'. Paul Johnson adds:

> At night, in winter, the infernal landscape could be seen at its most exciting: flames
> and sparks leaping upwards out of the pot-banks, many only half a mile away,
> perhaps less, turning the clouds of smoke orange and pink, sometimes fiery red,
> the whole angry skyline seeming to heave with the frantic effort to burn and heat
> and scorch. I loved to watch it, this volcano nightscape, which I thought of as a
> natural phenomenon, not man-made. I stood on a chair, to see it better, my
> mother behind me. 'That is what Hell will be like,' she said solemnly, 'only worse.'

'Burslem in the 1930s' by Paul Johnson

Young Paul went with his father, who was head of the Burslem School of Art, on a visit to the Wedgwood works at Etruria.

> He took me round the showroom. 'Look at these new coffee pots and teapots. They call them Globes. They are designed by a genius called Norman Wilson, who is the manager of the works. Superb. This is a Bournvita jug and mug designed for Cadbury's. They have sold over a million of them. Beautiful, elegant, modern lines but no Picasso nonsense. Here's another fine coffee set designed by Keith Murray, a New Zealander, no harm in that. He's a good man too. This is a great age for design, Little Paul. Businessmen are at last beginning to recognise how important good design is. Look at this vase: it's called the Boat Race Vase. Designed by a brilliant artist called Eric Ravilious. There's a tea set designed by another clever young fellow, Rex Whistler. Here's a set with a garden implements design – Eric Ravilious again. And here's a piece of bad design: a coronation mug by an old friend, Laura Knight'.
> 'Why is it bad, daddy?'
> 'Oh, it's ostentatious, fussy, gaudy, too elaborate. Simplicity and elegance are what you should aim at.'

That last sentence could stand as a nutshell manifesto for Deco potters. The mention of the outstanding artists who worked for Wedgwood (two of them killed in the coming war) bears out what I suggested in my 'working definition' of Art Deco in 1968: 'Its ultimate aim was to end the old conflict between art and industry, the old snobbish distinction between artist and artisan, partly by making artists adept at crafts …' Johnson *père* was perhaps a little hard on Dame Laura Knight. She designed delightful circus scenes for Clarice Cliff (who also used designs by Graham Sutherland, Vanessa Bell, Duncan Grant and Frank Brangwyn) and for Foley (they too commissioned work by Vanessa Bell, Duncan Grant, and Brangwyn, as well as Paul Nash).

After Paul Johnson's visit to the Wedgwood works, his father told him:

> Change always brings losses. The Potteries is hideous, dirty, wasteful and, I suppose, inefficient these days. But it's beautiful. Your mother doesn't see it. Nor do most people. But I do and you do, Little Paul. The French have a word for it – *jolie laide*. The Potteries is an ugly woman who has a strange kind of beauty. I shall be sorry when they kill her off.'

Nearly half a century later, Paul Johnson revisited the Potteries.

> All had changed [he writes]. The smoke, the soot, the smog and fog had gone. The coalmines were still. The railways, except for one main line, had vanished. There seemed to be no heavy industrial activity at all. I saw no slums either. Most of all, a thousand bottle-shaped pot-banks, the main and essential ingredient of that unique landscape, had been demolished. One or two survivors formed an 'industrial museum'. Every element of dreary and uniform modernity had been introduced … The *jolie laide* had had a drastic facelift and was no doubt a happier creature in consequence. But in the process she had lost her strange, romantic beauty; and, I suspect, her soul.

The dark satanic mills may have gone; but the Deco ceramics survive, many of them as pristine as when they came out of the kiln like pearls rescued from oysters. It was the French cultural historian Champfleury (real name Jules Husson) who, in a book of 1867 on the fa ence made during the French Revolution, was moved to describe those wares in a Gallic hyperbole, as 'history frozen by fire'. Looking back, in 2005, over just about the same time-span as he was looking back – some 75 years – we may make a similar claim for the wares of Clarice Cliff, Susie Cooper and the other Deco ceramicists. With undimmed colour and untamed panache, they resurrect the *Zeitgeist* of their epoch.

BEVIS HILLIER, formerly editor of *The Connoisseur* and of *The Times* Saturday magazine, is the author of 28 books, including the three-volume authorised biography of Sir John Betjeman, Poet Laureate. He wrote the first English book on Art Deco in 1968; subsequently *The World of Art Deco* (1971) – the catalogue of a large Deco show in Minneapolis – and (with Stephen Escritt) *Art Deco Style* (1997). He advised Andy Warhol and Barbra Streisand on the formation of their Deco collections. Also among his books are three on ceramics: *Master Potters of the Industrial Revolution: The Turners of Lane End* (1965); *Pottery and Porcelain 1700-1914* (1969); and *Early English Porcelain* (1992). In 1975 he contributed an introduction to the book *Clarice Cliff* by Peter Wentworth-Sheilds and Kay Johnson; and he wrote the entry on Susie Cooper in the new *Dictionary of National Biography* (2004). He is a Fellow of the Royal Society of Arts and of the Royal Society of Literature.

AGE OF JAZZ

The 1920s and '30s are sometimes known as the Age of Jazz. Jazz developed in the early twentieth century; its roots are embedded in American popular culture. From about 1919 American jazz bands were visiting Britain and taking the country by storm. The contemporary perception of jazz was as novel, exotic and modern, and it inspired new forms of decoration, including continental and British ceramics.

Clarice Cliff may well have taken her inspiration for these wonderful *Age of Jazz* figures from some ceramic *Jazz Musician* figures, produced by the Parisian manufacturers Robj in 1925. She is also known to have been inspired by designs published in the French monthly journal *Mobilier et Décoration*. An issue of the journal published in 1929 showed some ceramic tree silhouettes by Robert Lallemant. Their method of production (pottery cut-outs) was very similar to that used by Clarice for her *Age of Jazz* figures.

1. 'AGE OF JAZZ' FIGURES

Clarice Cliff for A.J. Wilkinson
1930
Double figures height 21cms
Earthenware and hand-painted
Lent by Muir Hewitt

Clarice Cliff's toy-like and playful group was possibly made to be displayed around a 'wireless', when listening to dance-band music. These figures are now considered to be very evocative of the 1930s, but they were not popular at the time and did not sell well. They were difficult to manufacture because the flat cut-out shapes tended to warp in the kiln. This meant that there was a high proportion of unsaleable figures made, making them expensive items to produce. They are now very rare.

JAZZY POTS

The sources and varieties of Art Deco were so numerous that sometimes it seems to be not one style but many. You can see much of this variety in British Art Deco ceramics.

Susie Cooper's coffee set with geometric decoration was possibly inspired by European avant-garde painting. Exotic influences from China and Ancient Egypt can be seen on pots by Clews and Carlton. Sunrays, lightning flashes and streamlining all capture the spirit of the 1920s and '30s.

2. JAR AND COVER
Crown Devon
1930s
Height 43 cms
Earthenware, transfer printed, hand-painted
Lent by B. Meyer

Oriental-style jars and covers were very
fashionable in the inter-war years, and were
produced by a number of factories. This example
has a *Dog of Fo* (guardian of a Buddhist temple) on
the lid and is a version of the *Orient* pattern. The
stylish red and black decoration is emphasised by
zigzags and lightning flashes; these motifs were very
popular with European designers at the time.

3. GRAVY BOAT AND PLATE

Clarice Cliff for Newport Pottery
About 1936
Width 16.5 cms
Earthenware and hand-painted
Lent by the Potteries Museum & Art Gallery, Stoke-on-Trent

The plate and gravy boat are part of a dinner service. The shape is known as *Biarritz*, first introduced in 1933, and possibly influenced by the French designer Jean Luce. *Biarritz* was difficult to manufacture, as the plates tended to warp when fired. Consequently it was expensive to purchase, but still sold very well. The pattern, *Coral Firs,* was sometimes used to cover the whole plate in a bright painterly manner. On these examples the pattern is used in a more restrained fashion, making the objects seem less purely decorative and more functional.

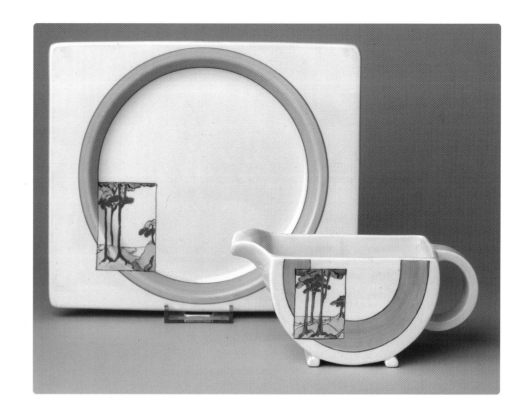

4. TEASET

Clarice Cliff for Newport Pottery
1930s
Teapot height 10.5 cms
Earthenware and hand-painted
Lent by Muir Hewitt

The modern and angular shape of the teaset is called the *Conical* shape and it is decorated with a pattern known as *Summerhouse*. The shape of the set is possibly derived from the work of Ilonka Karasz, a designer born and trained in Budapest. She designed a bowl in 1928, very like the *Conical* shape but made in silver plated metal. The *Conical* shape was introduced by Clarice Cliff in 1929 and the *Summerhouse* pattern in 1931.

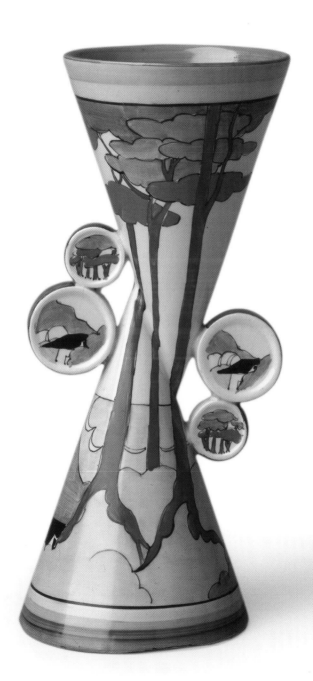

5. VASE
Clarice Cliff for Newport Pottery
1932-33
Height 24 cms
Earthenware and hand-painted
Lent by Muir Hewitt

Known as the *YoYo* vase this is one of the
boldest and most outrageous of Clarice Cliff's
designs. This vase is probably inspired by the
silver plated cocktail goblets created by the
French designer Desny in 1925. It is part of the
Fantasque range introduced in 1929 when
Colley Shorter decided to transfer some of the
sales to the adjoining Wilkinson factory. The
Bizarre range had proved to be so profitable
that he chose to create a new line. *Fantasque*
was sold at the same time as *Bizarre* but at
slightly higher prices.

6. CUP, SAUCER AND PLATE

Shelley
1930
Cup height 6.7 cms
Bone china, printed and enamelled
The Nick Berthoud Collection

28

This trio is in the *Vogue* shape, designed in 1930 by Eric Slater for Shelley. The modern geometric style attracted wide interest, with *The Pottery Gazette* commenting: 'They may or may not carry the public by storm, but one thing they certainly will do, they will cause people to stop and think … there are those who for a long time past have been agitating for a more adventurous spirit in the manufacturing circles of the pottery trade. Well here it is!' The public were not so impressed; the design was criticised for the solid handles, which made the cup difficult to hold, and the wide shape which made the tea cool too quickly. The shape was produced for less than three years.

The pattern which decorates the set is *Sunray*; five different *Sunray* colour-ways were used on *Vogue*. This very 'Deco' decoration complements the shape beautifully. The optimistic *Sunray* motif, with simplified geometric rays emanating from a semi-circular sun, was especially popular in Britain for garden gates, radios and in particular, stained glass windows in suburban front doors and porches.

7. VASE

George Clews & Co. Ltd.
1930s
Height 23.4 cms
Earthenware and hand-painted
Lent by Michelle Forster Davies

With its understated flame motifs this vase, from the *Chameleon Ware* series, shows an Egyptian influence. In 1922, the archaeologist Howard Carter excavated the tomb of the Egyptian boy king, Tutankhamun. By the mid '20s the symbols of Ancient Egypt were highly fashionable and were copied on to many pieces of pottery, jewellery and furniture. The decoration on this vase, although a watered down version compared to some pieces produced on the continent, is still quite stylish.

8. VASE

Carlton Ware
1930s
Height 25.5 cms
Earthenware, transfer printed and hand-painted
Lent by L. Adams

In the 1930s Carlton Ware took inspiration from many
different influences on their *Lustre Ware*. This vase has
Chinoiserie decoration — a style influenced by Chinese
decorative art and in this instance ceramics. Chinoiserie
has been popular in Europe since the 17th century.

9. PLATE

Carlton Ware
1930s
Diameter 32 cms
Earthenware and hand-painted
Lent by Muir Hewitt

This plate has a matt glaze and it is decorated with a
striking pattern of lotus flowers which are seen frequently
in Egyptian art. Carlton Ware made some very stylish and
diverse pots during the 1920s and '30s, constantly keeping
up with the demands of the British public.

10. BOX AND COVER

Susie Cooper for Gray's Pottery
Early 1930s
Width 13.1 cms
Earthenware and hand-painted
Lent by Nick Jones

This box and cover has sumptuous *Silver Lustre* decoration in the form of stylised flowers and leaves. Edward Gray began his factory in 1907. He did not manufacture his own wares but bought blanks from other manufacturers and decorated them. Susie Cooper (1902 - 1995) joined Gray's in 1922, first as a paintress and then as a designer.

11. COFFEE SET

Susie Cooper for George St. Pottery and Chelsea Works
About 1930
Coffee pot height 17.5 cms
Earthenware and hand-painted
Lent by Nick Jones

Susie Cooper was always aware of fashion and style. In this unusual coffee set with its flat stencil-like decoration Susie Cooper demonstrates her awareness of European avant-garde art of the period. The decoration on this set is very similar to paintings by the Russian Suprematist artist Kasimir Malevich (1878 - 1935).

12. CAT

Louis Wain
Design registered 1914
Height 12.7 cms
Earthenware and hand-painted
Lent by B. Meyer

Louis Wain (1860 - 1939) was famous for his drawings and paintings of cats. He designed this cat, whose geometric and angular form show the possible influence of Cubism – a style of painting where the subject is depicted simultaneously from multiple viewpoints, and its volume is expressed in terms of flat planes. This art movement began around 1908 and was led by Pablo Picasso (1881 - 1973) and Georges Braque (1882 - 1963). This cat figure could be a serious use of the Cubist style or a 'tongue-in-cheek' jokey reference. The painted marks on this cat's body are supposed to be symbols designed by Wain to represent the 'miaow miaow' cat sound.

13. VASE

Harold Stabler and Truda Adams for Poole Pottery
Late 1920s
Height 20 cms
Earthenware and hand-painted
The John Clarke Collection

This pot is a collaboration between Harold
Stabler (1872 - 1944) and Truda Adams (1890 -
1958). Economically decorated, Poole
demonstrates its ability to combine form and
decoration. A similar vase and pattern was
exhibited at the British Industries Fair in 1931.
Truda Adams/Carter designed many surface
patterns in the 1920s and '30s. She continued to
design for Poole until her retirement in 1950.

14. JUG
Wadeheath
1935
Height 19.2cms
Earthenware and hand-painted
Lent by Beverley

This jug, streamlined in design, has rather incongruous floral decoration. The shape seems influenced by speed or the prow of a ship. In the 1930s the British public had a fascination with speed and new modes of travel which were also reflected in some ceramics of the period.

15. VASE
Myott and Sons
1934-38
Height 22.1 cms
Earthenware and hand-painted
Lent by B. Meyer

Myott produced both traditional and modern tablewares. In the 1930s they responded to the public's taste producing this hand-painted fan-shaped vase, also made in other colour-ways. This was also made in response to the success of their competitors such as A.E. Gray and A.J. Wilkinson.

16 & 17. TEAPOTS

James Sadler and Sons
1934
Height 9 cms
Earthenware, transfer printed and hand-painted
16. Lent by L. Adams. 17. Lent by Beverley

Shaped novelty teapots were enormously popular in Britain and were widely collected. These two examples play on the form of a racing car. Although sculptural, they have a cosiness and sense of fun about them, demonstrating a humorous, very British reinterpretation of the images of speed often used in continental Art Deco design. The designer has rejected streamlining, speed and glamour in favour of a more rounded, homely shape. The registration plate reads OKT42, and some versions also have a hook-on sugar-bowl in the form of a caravan. Teapots like these were so popular that they were still made well into the 1950s, in various colour-ways. The teapot with applied transfer decoration shows how this model could be marketed specifically as *Nursery Ware*, while the green and lustre example is perhaps aimed at more adult taste.

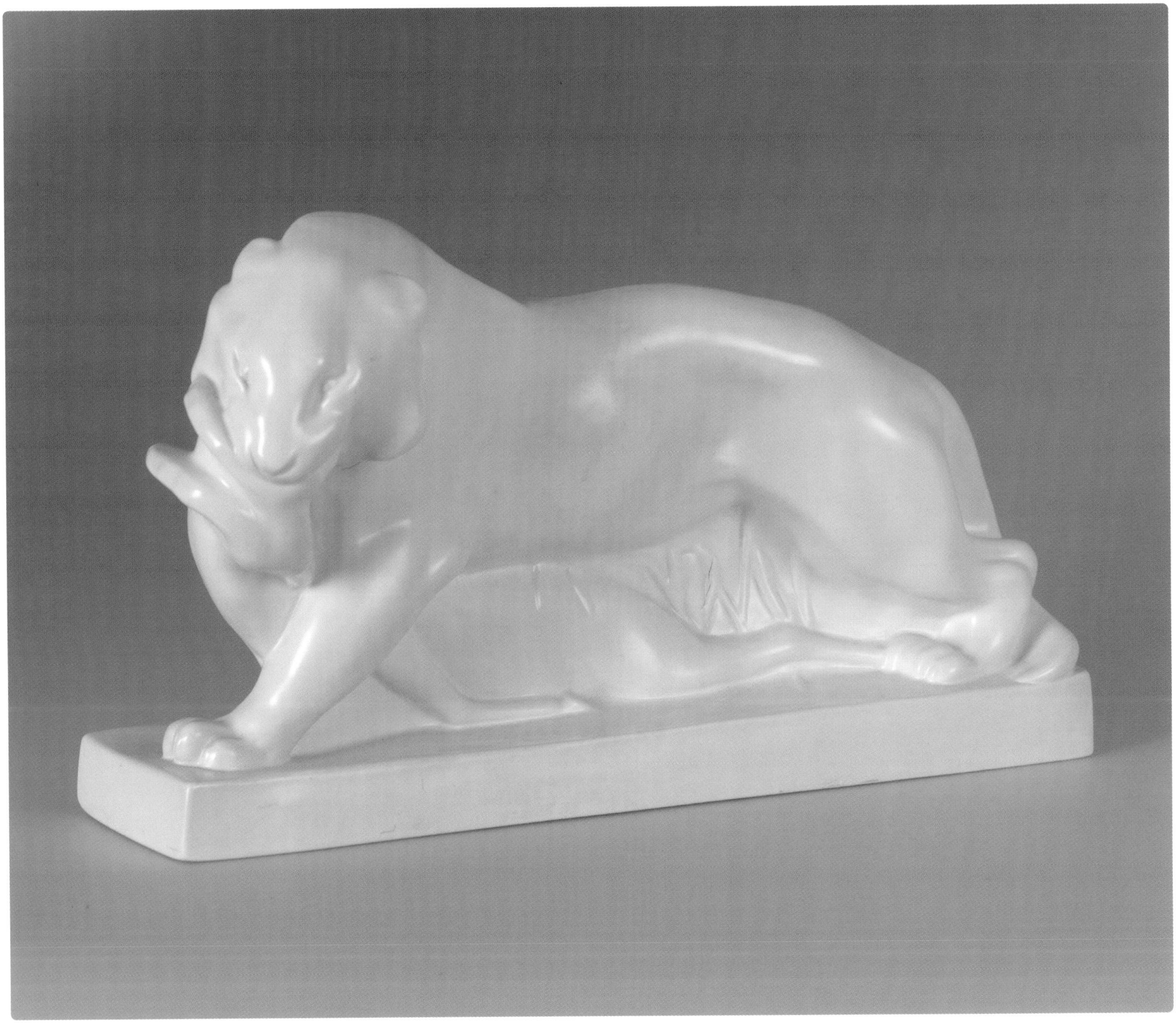

38

18. TIGER AND BUCK
John Skeaping for Wedgwood
1926
Height 19.7 cms
Earthenware
Lent by the Trustees of the Wedgwood Museum

The *Tiger and Buck* by John Skeaping (1901 - 1980) has a *Moonstone* glaze. He was taught to carve marble in Rome and married the sculptor Barbara Hepworth, who was to influence his work. His animals are modelled simply and yet they are bold and dynamic. *Tiger and Buck* was shown, in black basalt, at the 1933 British Industrial Art exhibition. Examples were on sale for over 23 shillings. Skeaping carved stone reliefs for the façade of the School for the Blind in Liverpool.

19. FIGURE
E.T. Bailey
About 1938
Height 16.6 cms
Earthenware
Lent by the Potteries Museum & Art Gallery, Stoke-on-Trent

The man on the motorbike was modelled by E.T. Bailey when at the Art School in Burslem. It has a glaze containing copper which gives it a rich and interesting appearance. The bike and rider are modelled as a single shape, suggesting their appearance at high speed. Motorbikes were considered a very daring and exciting means of transport in the 1930s.

THE PAINTRESSES

The Paintresses represented here are Clarice Cliff (1898 - 1972), Susie Cooper (1902-1995) and Charlotte Rhead (1885 - 1947), who all played their part in British Art Deco ceramics design in the 1920s and '30s.

There were scores of women painters working in the ceramic industry in Britain at this time, many of whom had lost their husbands, fathers or sons in the First World War. These women came from a variety of backgrounds and they had to struggle to succeed in a male dominated profession. Some women worked for just one pottery, others worked freelance, while others worked for more than one company. Some of the young girls and women who decorated the ceramics had learnt their skills either as apprentices or at the local Art Schools and most received no recognition for their work.

What sets Clarice, Susie and Charlotte apart was the fact that they were all highly regarded and recognised as talented designers in their day and, as a testament to that, their names were used as marks on their wares. Clarice Cliff rose through the ranks firstly as a decorator for A.J. Wilkinson Ltd. in 1916, to becoming the company's Art Director in 1931. She designed many stunning and innovative shapes and patterns at Wilkinsons. She married the owner of the company, Colley Shorter, and after his death in 1963 she sold the firm and retired.

Susie Cooper joined A.E. Gray's decorating firm in 1922 and by 1929 she had started her own company. She, like Clarice Cliff, was one of only a few women to design the shapes of some of her wares as well as the decoration. Her first designs were bright and often heavily painted but she went on to design in a more simple and restrained manner. Her company was acquired by the Wedgwood group in 1966 but she continued to design up until her death.

Charlotte Rhead, unlike Clarice and Susie, was born into a family of designers. She worked for a number of companies including Wood & Sons, Burgess and Leigh, A.G. Richardson and H.J. Wood designing mostly tube-lined patterns. She was not an entrepreneur like Clarice and Susie, and some of her designs are more rooted in the past but nevertheless she was highly regarded in the 1920s and '30s and she takes her place here as one of the Paintresses.

20. 'TEA FOR TWO' SET
Clarice Cliff for Newport Pottery
1930
Teapot height 12 cms
Earthenware and hand-painted
Purchased with the assistance of the Friends of the
National Museums Liverpool

In 1930 Clarice designed this stunning set that included a new teapot shape inspired by a silver pot by Jean Tétard, the French silversmith. An image of this teapot, produced for Tétard Frères was shown in the French monthly journal *Mobilier et Décoration* in 1930. Translating an Art Deco metal form into clay was not an easy task but Clarice managed the transformation, changing only the handle. The teapot became known as the *Stamford* shape and proved a winner, even in the dreadful economic climate of the 1930s. Colley Shorter had to purchase the rights to Tétard's design when Tétard realised that Clarice had copied it. The cups and saucers are of the *Conical* shape, a form already used by Clarice in the late 1920s. The hand-painted design is known as *Blue Autumn* and is one of the rarer Autumn colour-ways produced.

21. VASE

Clarice Cliff for Newport Pottery
1930s
Height 18.5 cms
Earthenware and hand-painted
Lent by Muir Hewitt

Known as the *Flower Tube* this vase has an 'S' shaped fin supporting
a tube on either side. This is the second version, as the original vase
just had one tube for flowers. It was decorated with a number of
patterns in the '30s and this is a *Summerhouse* version.

22. COFFEE POT

Clarice Cliff for Newport Pottery
1933-34
Height 18.5 cms
Earthenware and hand-painted
Lent by Lin Byrne

Clarice Cliff was again influenced by the designs of
Jean Tétard, the French silversmith. The shape, known
as *Bonjour*, is inspirational and it is to Clarice's credit
that she once again translated a metal shape into clay.
The pattern is known as *Windbells* and on one side
are foxgloves. Unexpectedly, on the other side is
painted a very stylised tree.

23. CHARGER

Clarice Cliff for A.J. Wilkinson Ltd.
About 1931
Diameter 45.5 cms
Earthenware and hand-painted
Lent by B. Meyer

This is a highly unusual and rare charger. Known as *Inspiration* this kind of ware was expensive to produce because of the mixture of glazes and decoration. The pattern of a knight on horseback by a stone wall is known as *Knight Errant* – a medieval knight in search of chivalrous adventures. Issued in 1931, it did not sell well.

24. WALL PLAQUE

Clarice Cliff for A.J. Wilkinson Ltd.
Late 1930s
Height 42 cms
Earthenware and hand-painted
Lent by Jill and Mike Newsham

This rare wall plaque is a part of the *My Garden* series, and one of a pair. The moulded flowers are familiar, and can be seen on the *Flora* facemasks. Although very decorative and charming, this plaque does not have the dynamism of Clarice's earlier work. However, to Clarice's credit, she was responding to changing public taste in the late 1930s.

25. VASE

Charlotte Rhead for Bursley Ware
1930s
Height 22 cms
Earthenware, hand-painted and tube-lined
Lent by the Potteries Museum & Art Gallery, Stoke-on-Trent

In the *Pomona* pattern, this vase has an intricate pattern with
pomegranates, flowers and grapes on a mottled ground. Charlotte
Rhead is particularly associated with the decorative technique known as
tube-lining – whereby the creamy coloured slip (liquid clay) is piped on
to the piece before firing. Various coloured enamels are then applied
and it is fired again. This is a very labour intensive method of
decoration; it meant that the pieces were expensive to produce and
were often sold as more luxurious items.

26. CHARGER

Charlotte Rhead for Crown Ducal
About 1935
Diameter 43.9 cms
Earthenware, hand-painted and tube-lined
Lent by the Potteries Museum & Art Gallery, Stoke-on-Trent

This charger, with its earthy coloured decoration, is
more abstract and European in influence than some of
Charlotte Rhead's other designs. It would have sat
comfortably in an interior furnished in a more
continental style of the '30s.

27. VASE
Charlotte Rhead for Crown Ducal
1930s
Height 22 cms
Earthenware, hand-painted and tube-lined
Lent by Beverley

With the *Persian Rose* pattern this traditionally shaped vase
is typical of Charlotte Rhead's designs in the 1930s. Unlike
the work of Clarice Cliff and Susie Cooper, Charlotte
Rhead's patterns are often more rooted in the Arts and
Crafts Movement than the 'Age of Jazz'. However, they seem
to blend with modern British styles of the time.

28. CHARGER
Charlotte Rhead for Crown Ducal
1939
Diameter 43.5 cms
Earthenware, hand-painted and tube-lined
Lent by Lynne G. Cottrell

This charger, in the *Trellis* pattern with its muted
tones, is reminiscent of some of the textile
designs of the period. It would have blended
easily into most British homes in the late 1930s.

46

29. COFFEE SET
A Susie Cooper Production for Crown Works
1930s
Height of coffee pot 19 cms
Earthenware and hand-painted
Lent by the Potteries Museum & Art Gallery, Stoke-on-Trent

Known as the *Kestrel* shape, this stunning coffee set was made as part of a practical and functional range, which was unveiled in 1932. Susie Cooper had the knack of designing in a very modern and understated manner in the 1930s. The decoration is simplicity itself and proved a winner with *Kestrel* shaped wares remaining in production for almost thirty years.

30. TEASET
A Susie Cooper Production for Crown Works
About 1932
Teapot height 16.5 cms
Earthenware and hand-painted
Lent by Nick Jones

Decorated with the *Galaxy* pattern this part teaset is not only hand-painted but also has some very subtle decoration in the form of *scraffito* – a pattern scratched through the surface to reveal the colour underneath. Throughout Susie Cooper's career she experimented with different forms of decoration. Robust and with an abstract pattern this set is simply known as the *Cube* shape.

31. VASE
A Susie Cooper Production
1931
Height 15 cms
Earthenware and hand-painted
Lent by Nick Jones

Susie Cooper has managed to combine images of
the modern machine age with this clean and
crisp cogwheel pattern on a piece inspired by
ancient Peruvian pottery. Known as *Console* this
vase is, up to now, the only known example of
this shape and pattern. Timeless in design, this is
one of Susie Cooper's finest pieces.

32. VASE
A.E. Gray and Co., Ltd.
1925
Height 19.2 cms
Earthenware and hand-painted
Lent by Nick Jones

Conventional in shape this brightly coloured vase was part of a range known as *Gloria Lustre* and was possibly designed by Susie Cooper. A selection of lustre designs was shown at the British Empire Exhibition of 1924, and the Paris Decorative Arts Exposition in 1925. These included some fruit and floral patterns by Susie Cooper. The hand painted decoration on this pot looks very European, possibly inspired by French metalwork.

33. VASE
A. E. Gray and Co., Ltd.
1925
Height 30.5 cms
Earthenware and hand-painted
Private Collection

Decorated with copper and mother of pearl lustre, this vase is a stunning example of *Gloria Lustre*; a range that was first introduced by A.E. Gray in 1923. The vase dates from the mid-1920s, and the decoration with its stylish running antelopes and orange tree was probably designed by Susie Cooper. She joined A.E. Gray in 1922 and stayed until 1929. It was hand-painted by Hilda May Lockett.

FIGURES

Free-standing Art Deco figures were less commonly made in Britain than on the Continent. As figures were more expensive to produce than tablewares, few factories produced them.

Doulton, however, produced some very good quality and well modelled figures as did Minton with the *Bather*, modelled by Doris Lindner. Jessie Van Hallen at Wade was a prolific designer and her very stylish *Christina* figure, coated with a cellulose spray, was made for the cheaper end of the market. *Christina* could easily have been inspired by the luxurious and expensive chryselephantine figures made on the Continent from patinated bronze and ivory and designed by Demetre Chiparus and Ferdinand Preiss.

Figurative subjects were also used to great effect on plates and ceramics with flat surfaces including the running *Leipzig Girl* made at the Poole Pottery and the three sided lamp base, with its *Clown* decoration by Susie Cooper.

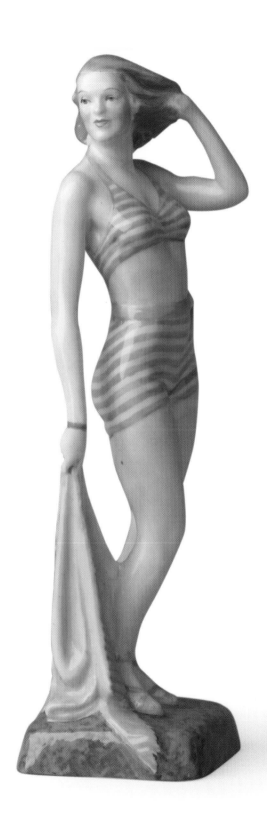

34. THE BATHER
Doris Lindner for Mintons
About 1935
Height 19.8 cms
Bone china and hand-painted
National Museums Liverpool

This delightful and rare figure of the *Bather* is by
Doris Lindner, who is better known as a modeller
for the Royal Worcester Factory. Lindner trained
at St. Martin's School of Art in London and the
British Academy School in Rome. The figure of
the lady with her matching beach clothes
manages to look simultaneously both wholesome
and coquettish.

35. JUG

Clarice Cliff for Newport Pottery
1930s
Height 16.6 cms
Earthenware and hand-painted
Lent by B. Meyer

This very Art Deco shaped *Conical* jug has a
particularly incongruous pattern of a lady in a
crinoline dress in a garden setting. Tellingly the
pattern is called *Idyll*. The crinolined figure was used
in Britain throughout the 1930s, and appears on
many items from tea-wares to embroidered tea-
cosies and tablecloths. The British favoured this type
of design possibly because it looked back to a bygone
age that was perceived as comfortable and romantic
and so this jug is an interesting mixture of the very
modern and the nostalgic.

36. CANDLESTICK

Clarice Cliff for Newport Pottery
About 1935
Height 18.0 cms
Earthenware and hand-painted
Lent by Jill and Mike Newsham

By the mid-1930s ceramics with moulded decoration
had become very fashionable. Clarice Cliff responded
by producing this candlestick known as *Girl* which is
part of the *My Garden* series.

37. ASHTRAY

Clarice Cliff for A.J. Wilkinson Ltd.
1930s
Height 16.5 cms
Earthenware and hand-painted
Lent by L. Adams

Ashtrays, by this time, were an everyday object in most British homes. It was now acceptable, and even fashionable, for women to smoke. This ashtray, with its figure of a stylish young lady, and its exotic name *Lido Lady*, gave it a fashionable air. A lido is a public open-air swimming pool or pleasure beach and these were increasingly available to the public during the 1930s.

38. JUG
Burleigh Ware
1933
Height 20 cms
Earthenware and hand-painted
Lent by L. Adams

This bold and elaborately moulded *Guards* jug is a considered and clever design. This variation was produced in three colour-ways, but it was only produced for a short time as, surprisingly, it did not sell well. Burgess and Leigh also produced 27 types of yellow glazed flower jugs of different types. They were modelled by Ernest Tansley Bailey, and were widely popular. Harold Lowe used antimony to design the distinctive yellow glaze that is found on all these products.

39. JUG
Burleigh Ware
1934
19.5 cms
Earthenware and hand-painted
Lent by B. Meyer

The *Golfer* jug was first issued in 1934. This was the first of a series of *Sportsman* jugs made by Burgess and Leigh. This range also included a Cricketer and Tennis Player and proved to be very popular.

40. SAILOR
Crown Ducal
About 1933
Height 22.5 cms
Earthenware and hand-painted
Lent by Muir Hewitt

41. CLOWN
Crown Ducal
About 1933
Height 21 cms
Earthenware and hand-painted
Lent by B. Meyer

Made as part of a series, these figures of a *Sailor* and a *Clown* are quite rare. A *Golfer* is also known to exist. Well modelled, painted with brightly coloured enamels and with a jaunty air, both figures show a continental influence and are great fun.

42. GUAN YIN

Unmarked
1919-22
Height 15.9 cms
Bone china and hand-painted
Lent by Nick Jones

Susie Cooper made this figure of *Guan Yin*, the Chinese
Goddess of Mercy, when at the Burslem School of Art from
1919. The course that she attended included woodcarving
and stained glass, but she had little formal training in
ceramics. She did, however, display considerable modelling
skills that are demonstrated here with this charming figure.

43. PLATE

A Susie Cooper Production for Crown Works
About 1936
Diameter 25.4 cms
Earthenware and hand-painted
Lent by Nick Jones

This *Moustache* plate was made as a sample. It is hand-painted, and this model would have been used as the basis for a lithograph – a form of transfer print – which was used to decorate mass produced items, in this case *Moustache* cups and saucers. These pieces were particularly popular in America. It is reasonable to suppose that Susie Cooper painted this sample piece herself.

44. LAMP BASE

A Susie Cooper Production for Crown Works
About 1932
Height 12.8 cms
Earthenware and hand-painted
Lent by Nick Jones

This rare triangular shaped lamp base is decorated with a clown, a popular image on ceramics of the period. It was first shown at Susie Cooper's trade stand at the British Industries Fair of 1932. According to the *Pottery Gazettte* '… the Queen and her party made purchases from the stand. The Princess Royal (Princess Mary and Countess of Harewood) purchasing a *Clown Lamp Base*'.

45. FIGURE

Jessie Van Hallen for Wade
1930s
Height 29 cms
Earthenware and hand-painted
Lent by Beverley

Trained at the Burslem School of Art and West
Ham Polytechnic, Jessie Van Hallen (1902 - 1993)
designed this figure known as *Christina* as part of
a series. Her figures are quite distinctive because
of their sense of movement and this one has a
more continental than British feel to it. The
figures are now quite rare as they have a
cellulose spray finish and many of them have
deteriorated badly over the years.

46. FIGURE

R.H. & S.L. Plant
1930s
Height 22 cms
Bone china and hand-painted
Lent by Lyn Ramsdale

Plant is a firm more usually associated with
tableware but in the 1930s, responding to public
demand, they went on to produce what were known
in the trade as *Novelties*. This figure is known as the
Cossack's Daughter and is part of a series.

47. FIGURE

Mabel Lucie Attwell for Shelley
About 1937
Height 16 cms
Bone china and hand-painted
Lent by Beverley

Known as *I'se going Ta Ta,* this pudgy-cheeked
child was designed by the famous illustrator
Mabel Lucie Attwell (1879 - 1964). She devised a
successful range of nursery ware for Shelley from
1926, and went on to design these popular
figures in the 1930s.

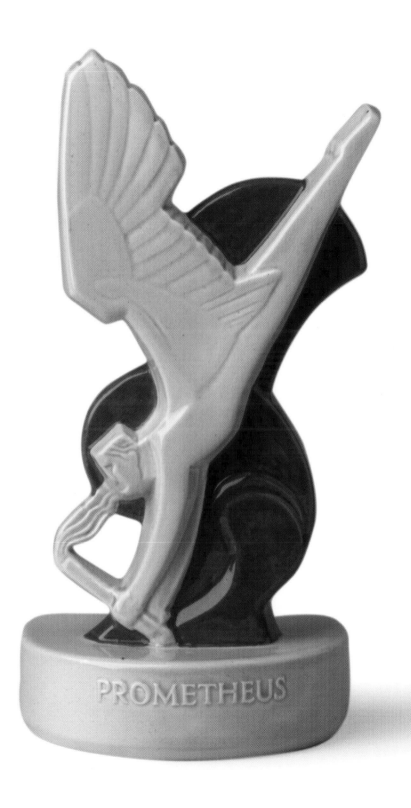

48. PROMETHEUS
Percy Metcalfe for Ashtead
About 1925
Height 19.5 cms
Earthenware and hand painted
The Nick Berthoud Collection

This piece was made as an advertisement for Hope's Heating and Lighting Ltd. It was designed by Percy Metcalfe (1895 - 1970) for the Ashtead Potters and shows part of a Greek myth. The Titan Prometheus stole fire from the Gods on Olympus to give to his creation – the human race. This went against Zeus's orders (he did not want them to have fire), and as a terrible punishment Prometheus was chained to a rock for all eternity. Every day a vulture came to peck out his liver, and every night his liver renewed itself. Luckily we do not see this part of the myth, instead the figure shows Prometheus hurrying down from Olympus to hand over the precious fire to mankind.

Hope's were a long established firm who supplied gas and solid fuel appliances. It may be that their advertising was aimed at counteracting the rise of electric power. Electricity's future in the home was secured in 1926, when the Electricity Supply Act established the National Grid – still powering us today.

49. SHELLEY GIRL

Shelley
1925-26
Size 30.5 cms
Bone china and hand-painted
Lent by Beverley

When Wileman and Co. decided to change their
company name to Shelley in 1925, a Mr. Smedley
and his agency were employed to handle their
advertising. Known as the *Shelley Girl*, this
fashionable figure was produced to appear in shop
displays across the country. She was used to
demonstrate how stylish tea drinking could be, and
how much more so when drunk from a Shelley
cup and saucer. Shelley adverts emphasised the
high standard of their goods and encouraged
customers to consider quality before price. The
company became known for their innovative styles
and patterns and maintained their business and
profile through the Depression era.

50. CHARGER
Poole Pottery
Late 1920s
Diameter 45 cms
Earthenware and hand-painted
The John Clarke Collection

This charger was made from a red earthenware
and painted by Margaret Holder on a clear glaze
over a white slip, to a design by Olive Bourne. The
decoration is known as the *Leipzig Girl* because a
similar dish was shown at the International
Exhibition of Industrial Art in Leipzig in 1927.

LAND & SEASCAPES

Land and seascapes figure largely as subject matter on British Art Deco ceramics, possibly because they are easily adapted to most pot shapes. Clarice Cliff probably used them more than any other designer in the 1920s and '30s. Her designs have a certain British cosiness about them, but by combining them with sharply Continental shapes and vibrant hand-painted decorations, she gave them great vitality.

Other designers such as Donald Gilbert at Denby gave the subjects a more abstract feel, whilst Crown Devon embraced the fairy-tale elements of landscapes with sumptuous patterns, colour and gilded decoration.

51. DISH

Crown Devon
1930s
Width 31.5 cms
Earthenware, transfer printed and hand-painted
Lent by L. Adams

Part of the *Mattajade* range, this traditionally shaped dish is decorated with a pattern known as *Fairy Castle*. It is decorated sumptuously in a style possibly inspired by book illustrations of the period. Pure fantasy, the castle could be the home to Sleeping Beauty. Castles were used as motifs by other designers of the period, including Clarice Cliff and Jean Luce.

52. PLATE

Reginald Haggar for Minton
About 1930
Diameter 22.8 cms
Earthenware, transfer printed and hand-painted
The Nick Berthoud Collection

Reginald Haggar (1905 - 1988) became the Art Director
of Minton in 1930 after his training at Ipswich School of
Art and the Royal College of Art, South Kensington, where
he studied pictorial design. The pattern on this plate is
known as *Modern Art* and is restrained yet playful.

53. PLATE

Reginald Haggar for Minton
About 1930
Diameter 20 cms
Earthenware and hand-painted
The Nick Berthoud Collection

Known as *Sailing Ships* this pattern was designed
by Reginald Haggar. It is simple and stylish like
many of his designs. Haggar was devoted to the
Potteries and was not only a designer but a
renowned researcher, writer and lecturer.

66

54. COFFEE POT

Crown Ducal
About 1925
Height 17.5 cms
Earthenware, transfer printed and hand-painted
Lent by the Potteries Museum & Art Gallery, Stoke-on-Trent

This coffee pot has a pattern known as *Red Tree*, also known today as *Orange Tree*. It took the pottery industry by storm in the 1920s because of its economical and clever use of pattern. It was the first of the tree silhouette designs and set a vogue for dainty teaware. It proved to be an extremely popular line and continued in production for many years.

55. TILES
Alfred Bawden for Carter and Co.
Late 1920s
Width 15.3 cms
Earthenware and hand-painted
National Museums Liverpool

Part of a *Sporting* series, these tiles were designed by Alfred Bawden who designed for Carter and Co., whilst still a student at the Royal College of Art. They were made from 1922 up to the 1950s as they proved to be a very popular design.

56. JAR AND COVER

Wm. Moorcroft
1928
Height 19 cms
Earthenware, tube-lined and hand-painted
Lent by W. Moorcroft PLC, Burslem, Stoke-on-Trent

Decorated with a pattern known as *Dawn* this is a traditionally shaped jar and cover. What made this piece fashionable, at the time, is the smudged painterly quality of the landscape, and the chevron patterned border.

57. VASE

Wm. Moorcroft
1934 - 1938
Height 22.5 cms
Earthenware, tube-lined and hand-painted
Lent by W. Moorcroft PLC, Burslem, Stoke-on-Trent

This vase is handmade and decorated with the simple *Yacht* pattern. The pattern can also be found in other colour-ways on dinner and tea wares. It is much simpler than many of the patterns traditionally associated with Moorcroft, but like some of the other ceramic manufacturers in the 1930s, they were responding to changing public taste. However, some of the simpler patterns produced by Moorcroft were not well received as they were not considered typical of the factory's usual production.

58. VASE

Donald Gilbert for Denby
About 1933
Height 13.6 cms
Stoneware
The John Clarke Collection

The artist and sculptor Donald Gilbert (1900 - 1961) designed this vase. It has a sumptuous glaze and is part of a series known as *Pastel Blue*. All the shapes in the range were named after places in the Lake District. This pot with its moulded form evokes the impression of a landscape and was possibly known as *Kendal*.

59. ADVERTISING PLAQUE
Clarice Cliff
1936
Height 6 cms
Earthenware and hand-painted
The Nick Berthoud Collection

Plaques of this type were used as advertising samples to show prospective buyers, in stores, the new designs and colour-ways available. These plaques – now rare – would have helped the factory identify which patterns would sell to the general public, ensuring that production could be targeted on potentially profitable lines. This is hand-painted on the reverse, identifying the pattern as *Brookfieds* (sic) by Clarice Cliff.

60. PLATE
Clarice Cliff for Newport Pottery
About 1931
Diameter 22 cms
Earthenware and hand-painted
Lent by Beverley

The pattern known as *Gibraltar* shows yachts, with the Rock of Gibraltar in the background. The pattern works well painted in pastel colours evoking the atmosphere of the Mediterranean. First introduced in 1931, this pattern would have been cheerful to use at the tea table during the dark days of the Depression.

61. CHARGER

Clarice Cliff for Newport Pottery
1931
Diameter 45.5 cms
Earthenware and hand-painted
Lent by Muir Hewitt

This striking looking charger has an intentional
hand-thrown quality. With its *Honey* glaze and
vibrant colours in the *Blue Autumn* pattern, it
would have added a touch of style to any
interior of the period. This pattern was produced
in other colour-ways including *Red Autumn*, *Pastel
Autumn* and *Orange Autumn*.

62. SANDWICH PLATE

Clarice Cliff for A.J. Wilkinson Ltd.
About 1936-37
Width 30 cms
Earthenware and hand-painted
Lent by Jill and Mike Newsham

This charmingly painted pattern known as *Chalet* shows a form of decoration known as *Café au Lait*. The stipple effect was used earlier in the 1930s and then again on this range in 1936 and 1937. *Chalet* is a refined pattern and although beautifully painted is a watered down version, stylistically, of Clarice's earlier work.

63. VASE

Eric Ravilious for Wedgwood
1938
Height 26 cms
Earthenware, printed and hand-painted
Lent by the Trustees of the Wedgwood Museum

Looking like a giant egg cup, this vase is in the
Burslem shape and shows scenes from the Boat
Race. It is made from *Queen's Ware* – a creamy
coloured type of pottery first introduced by
Wedgwood in the 18th century. Eric Ravilious
(1903 - 1942) was not only a designer of
ceramics, but was also a wood engraver and
illustrator who brought both charm and humour
to his designs.

In 1940 Ravilious became an Official War
Artist and in 1942 he was sadly killed when flying
with Coastal Command.

74

64. PLATE

Keith Murray for Wedgwood
1934
Diameter 26.5 cms
Earthenware, hand-painted
Lent by the Trustees of the Wedgwood Museum

Not everything that Keith Murray (1892 - 1981) designed was undecorated, as is demonstrated by this pattern, known as *Green Tree* or *Weeping Willow*. Initially designing vases and other vessels for Wedgwood, he went on to design inexpensive tableware. The simple tree pattern is in green enamel and platinum on to a *Moonstone* glaze. Murray designed a number of different tableware patterns before designing the Savoy Hotel's china in platinum and green, with its monogram.

65. VASE

Alice Teichtner for Denby
1937
Height 19.8 cms
Stoneware
The Nick Berthoud Collection

Alice Teichtner designed this distinctive and
robust pot which was part of a series known as
Tyrolean. She was an Austrian artist and studio
potter who came to England at a time of unrest
in Europe and worked for the Denby factory, on
a freelance basis, from 1936. When war broke
out in 1939 she was forced to register as an
enemy alien. She emigrated to Canada in 1943.

66. JAR AND COVER
Susie Cooper for Gray's Pottery
about 1928
Height 23.4 cms
Earthenware and hand-painted
Lent by Nick Jones

This very conventionally shaped jar and cover, part of the *Moon and Mountains* range, uses visible brush strokes as part of the design. Susie Cooper, influenced by the Modernist Movement, designed a number of geometric patterns. However, she soon rejected these heavily enamelled wares as the decoration was easily scratched. She personally favoured her more restrained designs.

THE HARRODS CONNECTION

In 1934 Harrods store in London held a selling exhibition entitled 'Modern Art for the Table'. It was part of a Government campaign of the early 1930s to encourage leading artists to produce designs for industry, with the hope of improving ceramic and glass design. It was a ground breaking collaboration between the artistic community and the decorative arts industry.

Clarice Cliff was appointed the Art Director and twenty eight artists and designers were invited to submit their designs. Clarice and others translated these designs for painting and printing on to various ceramic and glass shapes. There were three companies involved: A.J. Wilkinson Ltd. produced the earthenware, E. Brain & Co. (Foley China) produced the bone china and Stuart and Sons the glass. Some designs were reproduced on specially designed shapes, others were put on to standard factory shapes.

Although some interesting pieces were produced, the experiment was not wholly successful. There was some critical acclaim but the general public was not overly enamoured by many of the pieces produced, as they were not what they wanted in the 1930s. Most of the ceramic patterns were discontinued after the exhibition.

67. PLATE

Duncan Grant for A.J. Wilkinson Ltd.
1934
Diameter 25.5 cms
Earthenware and hand-painted
Lent by Manchester City Galleries

Decorated with the *Poppy* pattern by Duncan Grant (1885 - 1978), this plate has a floral motif in a painterly style. Duncan Grant was a member of the Bloomsbury Group of writers and artists; his painting subjects tended to be of still-lifes, portraits and landscapes. Grant was also a co-director of the Omega workshops that had been set up by Roger Fry in 1913. Grant designed pottery, textiles, interior decoration and stage sets for Omega, using both the figurative and abstract styles. He lived at Charleston, in Surrey, with Vanessa Bell and they had a daughter Angelica. Both Vanessa and Angelica also designed ceramics for the Harrods Exhibition.

68. PLATE

Milner Gray for A.J. Wilkinson Ltd.
1934
Diameter 21.5 cms
Earthenware, transfer printed and hand-painted
The Nick Berthoud Collection

Decorated with the *Wavy Line* pattern, the design seems
timeless. Milner Gray (1899 - 1997) studied painting and
design at London University and Goldsmiths' College where
Graham Sutherland was a fellow student. He was a skilled
artist and designer who championed the marriage between
art and industry.

Milner Gray was appointed a Royal Designer for Industry
in 1938. He taught at the Royal College of Art, Goldsmiths'
College and the Chelsea School of Art, and received the
C.B.E. in 1968.

69. PLATE

Milner Gray for Foley
1934
Width 18.1 cms
Bone china
Lent by the Potteries Museum & Art Gallery, Stoke-on-Trent

This plate is simply and effectively decorated with the
floral pattern *Convolvulus*.

70. JUG

Milner Gray for Foley
1934
Height 8 cms
Bone china and transfer printed
The Nick Berthoud Collection

This jug is decorated with the *Old Mayfair* pattern. This
landscape pattern differs from the majority of wares produced
for the Harrods Exhibition. The picture depicted seems better
suited to a flat surface and does not sit particularly well on
the curved body of this jug.

71. PLATE
Gordon Forsyth for A.J. Wilkinson Ltd.
1934
Width 18.3 cms
Earthenware and hand-painted

72. PLATE
Gordon Forsyth for A.J. Wilkinson Ltd.
1934
Width 18.3 cms
Earthenware and hand-painted
Lent by the Potteries Museum & Art Gallery, Stoke-on-Trent

Gordon Forsyth (1879 - 1952) was an enormously influential figure in the ceramics industry, being amongst other things a painter, designer, teacher and writer. Earlier in the century he was the Art Director of Minton, Hollins and Co., before moving to Pilkingtons where he specialised in lustre decoration. He became Art Advisor to the British Pottery Manufacturers Federation and wrote extensively on the importance of art, design and training; advocating the synthesis of art and industry in the production of ceramics.

Gordon Forsyth was one of the most experienced ceramic designers to submit designs for the Harrods Exhibition. He designed these patterns for a dinner service on the *Biarritz* shape. These plates are first editions — each full dinner set was produced twelve times and marked with a 'First Edition' backstamp. This was not an original idea but was certainly a good advertising ploy. Subsequent production of each service depended on how well the first editions sold. Newspapers at the time reported that most of the first editions sold out before the opening of the exhibition. Virginia Woolf and Charles Laughton were amongst those who reserved first editions.

73. PLATE

Allan Walton for Foley
1934
Diameter 25.5 cms
Bone china and hand-painted
Lent by Jill and Mike Newsham

This plate, in the *Swirl* pattern was designed by
Allan Walton who studied at the Slade School of
Art and in Paris. He was a painter, designer,
decorator and architect. As Director of 'Allan
Walton Textiles' he was responsible for
commissioning some of the most enterprising
artist-designed screen-printed fabrics of the 1930s.

74. TEAPOT

Allan Walton for Foley
1934
Height 9.5 cms
Bone china and hand-painted
The Nick Berthoud Collection

This cheerful little teapot is in the *Mornington* pattern.
It was designed by Allan Walton. Walton was
interested in contemporary design, but Foley here
uses his pattern on a more traditionally shaped pot.

75. TEASET
Eva Crofts for A.J. Wilkinson Ltd.
1934
Teapot height 13 cms
Earthenware and hand-painted
The Nick Berthoud Collection

Eva Crofts (1875 - 1947) designed this freehand blue and silver band pattern on to a Clarice Cliff shape. She was the elder sister of Laura Knight. Not as talented as her sister, she did, however, design book covers and textile patterns for Donald Brothers.

76. PLATE

William Robins for A.J. Wilkinson Ltd.
1934
Diameter 23 cms
Earthenware and transfer printed
Lent by Jill and Mike Newsham

Decorated with the *Dolphins* pattern, this plate was
designed by William Robins (1882 - 1959). He trained
as an architect and later attended the St. Martin's
School of Art where he eventually became an
instructor. He was a prolific artist, author and
illustrator, particularly noted for his engravings. As a
member of the Royal Society of Painters, Etchers and
Engravers, he exhibited his work extensively. This
delicate pattern is reminiscent of the delicate lines
used in his etchings.

77. PLATE

John Armstrong for A.J. Wilkinson Ltd.
1934
Diameter 25.5 cms
Earthenware and hand-painted
The Nick Berthoud Collection

This plate is decorated with a pattern known as
Chevaux, or *Chaldean* and designed by John
Armstrong (1893 - 1973) in a traditional and
painterly manner. Chaldean means an inhabitant of an
ancient region on the Euphrates and Persian Gulf, and
it is an unusual name for the decoration.

Armstrong was a member of Unit One, a group
of painters, sculptors and architects that included Paul
Nash and Ben Nicholson. In the '30s Armstrong
designed for the ballet . He also designed costumes
for some of Korda's films such as the *Scarlet
Pimpernel* and *I Claudius,* before becoming a War
Artist in 1940.

78. PLATE

John Armstrong for Foley
1934
Diameter 16 cms
Bone china and hand-painted
Lent by Manchester City Galleries

This plate is designed with a circus scene of a bareback rider. Although attractive it was not as popular as
Laura Knight's *Circus* series.

85

79. TUREEN AND COVER

Dod Proctor for A.J. Wilkinson Ltd.
1934
Height 12 cms
Earthenware and hand-painted
The Nick Berthoud Collection

Painted with the *Marine* pattern this tureen and
cover is part of a dinner service designed by
Dod Proctor (1892 - 1972). Dorothy or 'Dod'
Proctor studied at the Forbes School of Painting
in Newlyn, Cornwall. She visited Paris and saw
paintings by Impressionist and Post-Impressionist
artists, such as Renoir and Cezanne, who
influenced her later work. While studying at
Newlyn she met the painter Ernest Proctor, they
married in 1912. During her time at Newlyn she
became friends with Laura Knight who also
designed for the Harrods Exhibition.

80. PLATE

Dod Proctor for Foley
1934
Width 18.3 cms
Bone china and hand-painted
Lent by the Potteries Museum & Art Gallery, Stoke-on-Trent

This plate was designed by Dod Proctor and is known
as the *Embroidery* pattern. Dod became famous in the
1920s when her painting, *Morning*, was purchased for
the nation by the *Daily Mail*. She was elected an
Associate Royal Academician in 1934, only the third
woman ever to reach that position.

81. PLATE

Ernest Proctor for A.J. Wilkinson Ltd.
1934
Diameter 22.5 cms
Earthenware and hand-painted
Lent by the National Museums & Galleries of Wales

The pattern on this plate is known as *Feather Leaves* and was designed by Ernest Proctor (1886 - 1935). He was an artist who studied at the Forbes School of Painting in Newlyn, Cornwall and in Paris. He is known for a variety of work including beach scenes, mystical figure and religious paintings. Married to the artist Dod Proctor, he sadly died in 1935, a year after the Harrods Exhibition.

82. BOWL

Ernest Proctor for Foley
1934
Diameter 12 cms
Bone china and hand-painted
Lent by the Potteries Museum & Art Gallery, Stoke-on-Trent

Designed by Ernest Proctor, this bowl has a hand-painted, banded and looped pattern.

83. PLATE

Graham Sutherland for A.J. Wilkinson Ltd.
1934
Diameter 22.5 cms
Earthenware and hand-painted
Lent by National Museums and Galleries of Wales

By Graham Sutherland (1903 - 1980), this plate is
decorated with small floral motifs. Graham Sutherland
was an artist who taught engraving at the Chelsea School
of Art and exhibited at the Royal Academy. He also
designed ballet costumes for Sir Frederick Ashton and
painted a number of portraits including W. Somerset
Maugham and Winston Churchill. Sutherland is also
famous for *The Christ in Glory* tapestry he designed for
Coventry Cathedral in 1960.

84. PLATE

Graham Sutherland for Foley
1933
Diameter 16.4 cms
Bone china, transfer printed and hand-painted
Lent by National Museums and Galleries of Wales

This plate is decorated with a pattern known as
English Rose. Designed by Graham Sutherland, it
comes in various colour-ways.

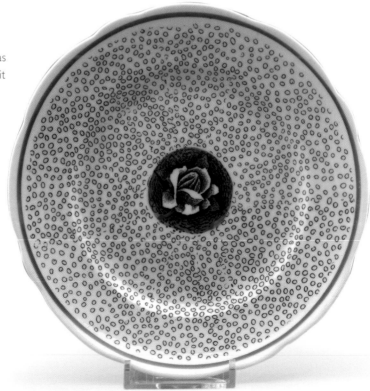

85. TEAPOT
Freda Beardmore for Foley
1934
Height 11.8 cms
Bone china and hand-painted
The Nick Berthoud Collection

Both the hand-painted teapot and plate are by Freda
Beardmore (d. 1977) who, as a young girl, attended the
Burslem School of Art. She joined Wedgwood as a
trainee designer in 1928 before going on to E. Brain
and Co., also known as Foley China.

86. PLATE
Freda Beardmore for Foley
1934
Diameter 13.2 cms
Bone china and hand-painted
Lent by the Potteries Museum & Art Gallery, Stoke-on-Trent

Freda Beardmore worked for E. Brain until the
outbreak of the Second World War when she became
an aeronautical inspector for Alvis, the motor company.
She was very much involved with the Harrods
Exhibition, not only because she submitted several of
her own designs but because she also helped adapt
some of the other artists' work for Foley.

87. LAMP BASE

Laura Knight for A. J. Wilkinson Ltd.
1934
Height 48.5 cms
Earthenware and hand-painted
Lent by L. Adams

Of all the designs for the Harrods Exhibition of 1934, Laura Knight's (1877 - 1970) were to prove the most successful. Laura Knight became enthralled with the big top when she followed a Carmo's circus group around in 1926 - 1927. The circus was run by the 'Great Carmo', born Harry Cameron, who worked with the famous circus owner Bertram Mills. She painted and drew aspects of circus life both in the ring and behind the scenes. These images became the inspiration for her range of ceramics for the Harrods exhibition.

Clarice Cliff and Joe Wooliscroft used their modelling skills to translate Laura Knight's sketches into this very striking lamp base. Part of the *Circus* series, this piece features clowns and acrobats balanced one on top of another. The *Circus* set was the only Harrods service to feature specifically modelled items, as well as the lamp base they produced a tureen, jug and teapot. The other sets designed for the exhibition made use of Wilkinson's existing shapes.

These plates are two examples from a full dinner service, all of which are decorated with variations of the *Circus* pattern. The first features a female bareback rider sitting on the rump of a piebald horse, the other a tightrope walker with a parasol. This was one of the services produced for the Harrods exhibition in 1934; it required a large amount of detailed work and hand painting and therefore was quite expensive to produce. Laura Knight was unusual in that she was fully engaged with the process of designing for ceramics. This interest was borne out in the public reaction to her designs; *Circus* was the most successful of the Harrods sets, despite its high price. Gracie Fields, one of the most popular entertainers in Britain at the time, is said to have bought a full set for £70.

Laura Knight was made a Dame in 1929 for her services to art and in 1936 became the first woman to be elected to the Royal Academy. Between 1939 and 1940 she was a war artist and in 1946 she attended the Nuremburg Trials as the official artist.

88 & 89. PLATES
Laura Knight for A.J. Wilkinson Ltd.
1934
Diameter 23 cms
Earthenware, transfer printed and hand-painted
Lent by the Potteries Museum & Art Gallery, Stoke-on-Trent

91

90. COFFEE POT
Laura Knight for Foley
1933
Height 17 cms
Bone china, transfer printed and hand-painted
Lent by National Museums and Galleries of Wales

91. PLATE
Laura Knight for Foley
1934
Diameter 18.5 cms
Bone china, transfer printed and hand-painted
Lent by Jill and Mike Newsham

This coffee pot and plate are painted with *Purple
Lustre* and decorated with the *Dove* pattern.
Laura Knight designed more than one pattern for
the Harrods exhibition, but this design, while
striking, was not as successful as *Circus*.

92. PLATE

Laura Knight for Foley
1934
Diameter 23 cms
Bone china and hand-painted
The Nick Berthoud Collection

Another pattern by Laura Knight, painted
freehand and known as *Cupid*.

FACE MASKS

African art was influential in the evolution of exotic Art Deco. Additionally, ceramic face masks, now closely associated with the 1920s and '30s, were possibly inspired by the African wooden masks imported into Britain at the time. Some ceramic manufacturers modelled masks on famous film stars such as Greta Garbo and Marlene Dietrich. Other factories such as J.H. Cope and John Beswick produced masks of fashionable young women often wearing jewellery and stylish hats.

Not all the masks were of women; Susie Cooper portrayed a *Judge* and a *Chinaman*. Clarice Cliff even produced a mask of the mythological god, *Pan*. Later on in the 1930s some of the masks were also made with a reservoir to contain water and flowers. All these masks would have looked stylish and modern in a British home between the Wars.

93 & 94. MASKS
Clarice Cliff
1930s
Height 16 cms
Earthenware and hand-painted
Lent by Jill and Mike Newsham

Clarice Cliff first introduced face masks, designed to be hung on the wall, in the late 1920s and they were produced over a ten-year period. Known as *Marlene*, this design was first produced in 1931 and was possibly based on Marlene Dietrich – the popular film star of the period. Here we have 2 versions of the same mask. Masks were popular and were produced until the late '30s.

95. WALL POCKET MASK

Clarice Cliff
1930s
Unmarked
Height 24 cms
Earthenware
Lent by Jill and Mike Newsham

This is a face mask with a difference as it has a reservoir to contain water and was intended to hold flowers. The face is that of Pan — the Greek god of woods and fields, flocks and herds, who charmed the nymphs with his pipe playing.

96 & 97. MASKS
Clarice Cliff
1930s
Height 18 cms
Earthenware and hand-painted
Lent by Jill and Mike Newsham

Flora is probably the best known of Clarice Cliff's face masks and was produced in two sizes and a choice of colours and glazes. The masks designed by Clarice Cliff were produced at the same time in both Newport Pottery and the A.J. Wilkinson factory. This means that masks, which are of the same period, and look the same, may be marked as being produced by different factories. It is thought that this strange practice was undertaken for tax reasons. Here we have the same mask in two different colour-ways.

98. WALL POCKET MASK

Clarice Cliff for A.J. Wilkinson Ltd.
Late 1930s
Height 18.5 cms
Earthenware and hand-painted
The John Clarke Collection

Yet another version of the *Marlene* face mask, but this one has an added reservoir to contain water and fresh or dried flowers.

99. MASK

Clarice Cliff for A.J. Wilkinson Ltd.
1930s
Height 13.7 cms
Earthenware and hand-painted
Lent by B. Meyer

This face mask is one of a series and was meant to be hung on the wall. Some of the series were also made in smaller sizes, with holes in the top so that they could be worn as pendants.

100. MASK
Susie Cooper
About 1933
Height 28.7 cms
Earthenware and hand-painted
Lent by Nick Jones

101. MASK
Susie Cooper
About 1933
Height 22 cms
Earthenware and hand-painted
Lent by Nick Jones

102. MASK *THE JUDGE*
Susie Cooper
About 1933
Height 29 cms
Earthenware
Lent by Nick Jones

103. MASK *THE CHINAMAN*
Unmarked
About 1933
Height 30.5 cms
Earthenware and hand-painted
Lent by Nick Jones

Susie Cooper produced four face masks for the wall, all of which are shown here. There are two female masks, one (100) is sometimes now known as the *Brunette* and is reputedly loosely modelled on Greta Garbo. The other (101) is sometimes known as the *Blonde* and is possibly a self-portrait, although Susie never confirmed that it was. The *Judge* is an undecorated version of the original, and is very unusual in this respect. Face masks of pretty and elegant ladies were popular during the 1930s. The four masks shown here, however imposing, would not have been considered attractive by most people. They were only made for a limited period and are therefore very rare.

104. MASK

J.H. Cope & Co. Ltd.
1930s
Height 19 cms
Earthenware and hand-painted
National Museums Liverpool

The firm of Cope produced tea wares for over sixty years, but they are better known for their range of face masks which were only made for a relatively short period. This mask, in a continental style, comes in a range of and shows a fashionable looking young woman.

105. MASK

Ashtead
1934
Height 23 cms
Earthenware
Lent by B. Meyer

This stylish mask is decorated with a vibrant *Daffodil* glaze. Ashtead produced a variety of functional and decorative wares, but are not widely known for their masks. It may be that these were a small sideline to boost sales in the difficult year of 1934, when many workers were forced to reduce their working hours. All production ceased at Ashtead in 1935, a year after this mask was produced.

106. PLAQUE
Unmarked
1936 - 1940
Height 31 cms
Earthenware and hand-painted
The John Clarke Collection

Made by Beswick this pretty plaque for the wall
is rather more elegant than some produced in
Britain in the '30s. Beswick produced many
pieces of pottery which are regarded in Britain as
Art Deco although they have little to do with
the international Art Deco style.

ANIMALS

Either as standing figures or decorative motifs, animal subjects are frequently part of the language of British Art Deco ceramics. There were many influences on Art Deco at the time. These include exotic species such as gazelles and antelopes from African art, as well as more homely but similarly elegant and streamlined animals like deer.

The artist Louis Wain used cats as inspiration for his very idiosyncratic figures possibly inspired by Cubist art. There were many different approaches to capturing the essence of animals in the 1920s and '30s, from the comic to the stylish.

There is a strong contrast between John Skeaping's animal forms, simplified to their sculptural essence, and a set of typical flying ducks which graced many a British home between the Wars. All have a part, however, in the story of British Art Deco ceramics.

John Adams for Poole Pottery
Late 1920s
Height 33 cms
Earthenware and hand-painted
The John Clarke Collection

This vase, with its *Leaping Deer* decoration, was designed by John Adams. He trained at the Royal College of Art and went on to develop his technical skills while working in Stoke-on-Trent in the tile industry, and at Bernard Moore's pottery, painting *Lustre Ware*. He understood how to combine art and industry. At Poole his designs were responsive to public taste and were very influential on the ceramic industry as a whole.

108. CAT

Louis Wain
Design registered 1914
Height 14.2 cms
Earthenware and hand-painted
Lent by B. Meyer

When Louis Wain's wife Emily became seriously ill he
drew their black and white kitten to amuse her. Emily
encouraged him to submit a picture to the *Illustrated
London News* and thereafter his pictures became more
and more sought after. It is said that because of Wain's
pictures, cats replaced dogs as Britain's number one
pet. He became fascinated by cats, and eventually he
became so obsessed by his creations he suffered a
nervous breakdown and was committed to the
Middlesex County Asylum in 1924.

109. LION

Louis Wain
Design registered 1914
Height 12 cms
Earthenware and hand-painted
Lent by B. Meyer

Although Louis Wain's ceramic cats are considered by
many to be Art Deco in style, they were first produced
as early as 1914. The Patent Office records show 'Max
Emanuel and Company, 41/42 Shoe Lane, London E.C.
China Manufacturer' as the holder of the patent for
the Wain cats. It is unlikely that Emanuel was a
manufacturer, and he is more likely to be a seller of
ceramic wares. The patent was renewed in 1919, which
implies that they were still produced at this time.

110. PLATE

Royal Cauldon
About 1930s
Diameter 35 cms
Earthenware, transfer printed and hand-painted
Lent by Muir Hewitt

This dramatic plate by Royal Cauldon depicts an image of the phoenix, which in mythology symbolises immortality and resurrection. Decorated in vibrant blues and reds, this plate embodies the spirit of the period and shows the designer's willingness to look at traditional subjects with a fresh and creative eye.

111. BOX AND COVER

Susie Cooper for Gray's Pottery
About 1929
Height 6.4 cms
Earthenware and hand-painted
Lent by Nick Jones

Deer, antelope and gazelle were popular subjects
for the Art Deco movement throughout Europe.
These motifs were used on a wide array of
objects from jewellery to architectural
metalwork. This box could have held all manner
of trinkets and mementos.

112. TABLE CENTRE

Susie Cooper for Crown Works
About 1936
Height of deer 20 cms
Earthenware and hand-painted
Lent by Nick Jones

As well as a deer, a fox and hound could also be
purchased to complement the set. The troughs were
made to contain flowers. The design was requested by
Gene Fondeville, Susie Cooper's New York agent. The
Leaping Deer, with its poise and grace, became a
signature design for Susie Cooper. It appeared as a
motif on many of her ceramics, and ultimately become
the backstamp on her pots.

113. FIGURE
Unmarked
1930s
21 cms
Earthenware
Lent by Muir Hewitt

This very strange and quirky animal was probably made to grace a nursery. One wonders, however, whether it would have given some children nightmares.

114. VASE
Wm. Moorcroft
1930s
Height 32.8 cms
Earthenware, tube lined and hand-painted
Lent by W. Moorcroft PLC, Burslem, Stoke on Trent

This eccentrically shaped vase is decorated sparingly with a *Fish* pattern. The fish float on a cream coloured background with an almost cartoon-like quality. Moorcroft in the 1930s produced a number of Fish patterns on different shapes and colour-ways.

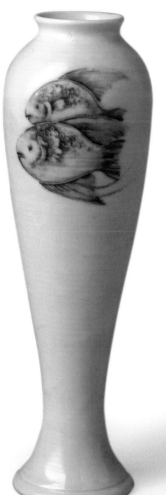

115. FLYING DUCKS
Unmarked
Probably 1930s
Height of large duck 12.7 cms
Earthenware and hand-painted
The Nick Berthoud Collection

What could be more reminiscent, to many
people, of the 1930s - '50s than this set of three
Flying Ducks? Produced by a number of factories
they graced many British homes at the time.
Regarded in this country nowadays as Art Deco,
they could not be more far removed from the
Deco produced on the Continent.

116. FLYING DUCK WALL POCKET
Unmarked
Probably 1930s
Height 28.5 cms
Earthenware and hand-painted
The Nick Berthoud Collection

This is a *Flying Duck* with a difference as it has a reservoir at the back to hold water and fresh or dried flowers.

117. HIPPOPOTAMUS PIPE STAND OR ASHTRAY

Clarice Cliff for A.J. Wilkinson Ltd.
About 1939
Height 9 cms
Earthenware and hand-painted
Lent by Jill and Mike Newsham

118. BIRD PIPE STAND

Clarice Cliff for A.J. Wilkinson Ltd.
About 1939
Height 8 cms
Earthenware and hand-painted
Lent by Jill and Mike Newsham

119. ELEPHANT ASHTRAY

Clarice Cliff for A.J. Wilkinson Ltd.
About 1939
Height 11.5 cms
Earthenware and hand-painted
Lent by Jill and Mike Newsham

Throughout her career, Clarice Cliff was interested in modelling and sculpture. From the 1920s onwards she designed some small, less expensive items known as 'Fancies'. Using her modelling skills she produced figures, bookends and wall plaques. These pieces were particularly saleable in the 1930s, even at a time of financial depression in Britain and they were an important source of revenue for the firm. They had a wide appeal and were often cute and so would not necessarily have appealed to those who were interested in her more avant-garde or outrageous designs.

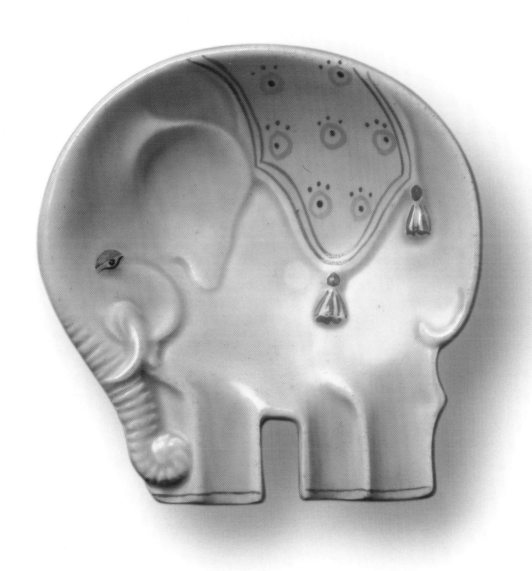

120. TEAPOT

Clarice Cliff for A.J. Wilkinson Ltd.
Late 1930s
Height 19.5 cms
Earthenware
Lent by the Potteries Museum & Art Gallery, Stoke-on-Trent

Known as the *Cockerel* teapot, this must have been great fun to use at the tea table. Novelties like this are not a 20th century invention, as teapots in unusual and exotic shapes have been around since the 18th century. However, novelty teapots underwent a renaissance during this period and were aimed at both adults and children.

121. CAT DISH

Clarice Cliff for Newport Pottery
1930s
Height 17 cms
Earthenware and hand-painted
Lent by B. Meyer

Designed as part of Clarice Cliff's *Nursery Ware* range, this dish is unusual as it stands on its side. This particular dish was used as a promotional piece and for display purposes.

114

122. FIGURE

Mabel Lucie Attwell for Shelley
About 1937
Height 7 cms
Bone china and hand-painted
Lent by Beverley

This little figure is part of a series of green-suited goblins, known as *Boo-Boos*, designed by Mabel Lucy Attwell. *Boo-Boos* had already been used by Attwell in 1920 as painted decoration on her nursery ware. This *Boo-Boo* was one of a series of eight stand-alone figures produced in the late 1930s. They show wit and whimsy, and must have been fun to collect – for adults, as well as children.

123. RABBIT

Unmarked
About 1928 - 1929
Height 12.5 cms
Stoneware
Lent by Jill and Mike Newsham

This rabbit is charmingly called Marmaduke and
was first produced in the late 1920s by Denby. It
is simple and stylised and was particularly liked
by children. Although this piece is unmarked it is
easily recognisable as Denby because of its
weight and robust quality. It was produced in
different sizes and also in a range of glazes. This
rabbit has a rare glaze known as *Cappuccino*.

124. MONKEY GROUP

Hugh Llewellyn for Poole Pottery
1920s
Height 16.5 cms
Stoneware
The Nick Berthoud Collection

Poole encouraged external artists and sculptors. This *Monkey Group* was modelled by Hugh Llewellyn, Headmaster at the Poole School of Art, in 1922-23, and was later released as a slip-cast group in a stoneware body.

125. TILES

E.E. Strickland for Carter and Co.
1930s
Width 15 cms
Earthenware
The John Clarke Collection

From a *Farmyard Series*, these tiles were designed by E.E. Strickland and were made by Carter and Co., a subsidiary of Carter, Stabler and Adams (Poole Pottery). Tiles were produced in large numbers in the 1920s and '30s, partly due to the increased emphasis on hygiene in public buildings, homes and shops. Considered not only decorative but also easy to clean, many food shops used tiles in their interiors, including butchers and fishmongers such as Dewhursts and MacFisheries.

126. SUGAR BOX AND COVER

Victor Skellern for Wedgwood
1935
Height 14.5 cms
Bone china and transfer printed
Lent by the Trustees of the Wedgwood Museum

While Victor Skellern's (1908 - 1966) approach to design and manufacturing was modern, unlike Keith Murray, Skellern was not a Modernist. He was particularly interested in patterned decoration, demonstrated here with this *Persian Ponies* sugar box from a teaset.

Victor Skellern became the Art Director for Wedgwood in 1934. He first introduced lithographic printing to Wedgwood through some of the first designs by Eric Ravilious.

127. PLATE

Victor Skellern for Wedgwood
1934
Diameter 22.5 cms
Earthenware and transfer printed
Lent by the Trustees of the Wedgwood Museum

The squirrel motif is one of the *Forest Folk* series. Designed on a celadon green body, this decoration, by Victor Skellern, was influenced by wood engravings and the countryside. He was often inspired by his surroundings whilst on holiday or walking in Derbyshire. The simplicity of the decoration is reminiscent of Danish pottery of the 1920s.

128. KANGAROO

John Skeaping for Wedgwood
1926
Height 23 cms
Earthenware
Lent by the Trustees of the Wedgwood Museum

This *Kangaroo* is one of ten animals first modelled by John Skeaping. It has a *Matt Straw* glaze by Norman Wilson. This series proved very appealing in the 1930s, as they were an inexpensive way to purchase modern pieces of industrially made sculpture for the home.

129. JAR AND COVER

Ashtead
1925
Height 9.8 cms
Earthenware
Lent by John Clark

Ashtead Pottery was founded in 1923 to give employment to ex-servicemen who had been disabled in the First World War. Buying from Ashtead could be seen as a particularly patriotic purchase, and the pottery was supported by Royalty and members of the Establishment. This jar is a commemorative piece, sold to tourists and day-trippers who visited the British Empire Exhibitions in 1924 and 1925. Several easily recognisable lion motifs advertised the exhibition, this jar bears the 'Herrick' Lion in the centre – this widely used exhibition emblem was applied to all types of wares sold by different companies. It was introduced for the 1924 exhibition, but was reused in 1925; this was a clever decision as it meant that goods left unsold in 1924 could be displayed as new in 1925. A huge range of souvenirs were sold to the public, and the Post Office celebrated the British Empire Exhibition by producing its first ever commemorative stamp.

FRUIT AND FLOWERS

Fruit and flowers have been the mainstay of English ceramic decoration for hundreds of years. These were subjects with a ready appeal and the English country garden had a wealth of inspiration for designers in the 1920s and '30s. Easily accessible, most people in Britain would have possessed something decorated with flowers. Whether it was a coffee set by Crown Ducal with its economical and banded *Red Tree* pattern, or a hand-painted vase by Radford, they would have cheered up many a British home.

From the factories' point of view, fruit and flowers were very appealing as subjects as they lent themselves easily to ceramic decoration.

130. COFFEE CAN AND SAUCER

Crown Devon
1920s
Height of cup 5.8 cms
Earthenware and hand-painted
National Museums Liverpool

The *Orient* pattern is of fine quality, and was introduced in the 1920s. It is one of the most stunning of Crown Devon's patterns, which was also applied to lamp-bases, ginger-jars and vases. This kind of ware was aimed at the top end of the market as it would have been expensive to produce, particularly with the amount of gilding that was applied.

131. VASE
Crown Devon
1930s
Height 19.8 cms
Earthenware, transfer printed and hand-painted
Lent by Beverley

Crown Devon is the trade name of Fielding &
Co., who have produced pottery since the 1870s.
This attractive vase with its *Floral Lustre*
decoration is similar to the pots produced by
Carlton Ware in the 1930s. This is possibly
because the designers, Enoch Wood and George
Baker, left the Carlton factory and joined Crown
Devon in 1930.

132. VASE

Clarice Cliff for A.J. Wilkinson Ltd.
Late 1930s
Height 19.5 cms
Earthenware and hand-painted
Lent by Jill and Mike Newsham

In 1934 Clarice Cliff began to produce a range of ceramics known as *My Garden*. These pieces were not as abstract or as exciting as some of her previous designs. However, this proved to be a very successful range as public taste was changing and, as ever, Clarice met the demand. This colour-way, *Midnight*, is one of the rarer varieties. The dark background emphasises the brilliant colours used to pick out the garden details.

133. TEASET
Clarice Cliff for Newport Pottery
1930s
Teapot height 12 cms
Earthenware and hand-painted
The Nick Berthoud Collection

Unlike some of Clarice Cliff's geometric patterns, this design, known as *Crocus*, is rather more traditional, whilst still retaining a certain verve. Perhaps this is because, in this instance, it is painted on the *Stamford* shape. The *Crocus* pattern became her best seller and has become known as her 'signature' pattern. As well as the more traditional shapes it was also painted on to the more geometric variety such as *Conical*. It was available in different colour-ways and variations including *Sunbeam*, *Spring*, *Peter Pan* and *Autumn Crocus*. The demand was so great that a separate *Crocus* workshop, employing up to thirty paintresses was established. The pattern sold well throughout Clarice's career, and was produced into the 1960s.

134. PLATE

Clarice Cliff for Newport Pottery
1930
Diameter 18 cms
Earthenware and hand-painted
Lent by Audrey Barr

Cubist in inspiration, this is one of Clarice Cliff's most successful abstract designs and is known as the *Melon* pattern. It was one of the few 'all over' designs produced in quantity for full tableware sets.

135. PLATE

Truda Carter for Poole Pottery
1930s
Diameter 28 cms
Earthenware and hand-painted
The John Clarke Collection

Taking its inspiration from plant forms, this abstract patterned plate is painted in muted tones and is very European in flavour. Truda Carter was experimenting with fewer colours, on a background of grey slip – clay watered down to a creamy consistency.

136. VASE
Truda Carter for Poole Pottery
1930s
Height 32 cms
Earthenware and hand-painted
The John Clarke Collection

This very rare and magnificent vase is by Truda
Carter (1890 - 1958). Designed in the late
1930s, it demonstrates with style and panache
the very best of British Art Deco ceramics and is
comparable to anything produced in France
between the Wars. Carter was previously
married to her fellow Poole designer John
Adams. She married Cyril Carter in 1931.

137. JUG
Unmarked
1930s
Height 21 cms
Earthenware and hand-painted
National Museums Liverpool

This jug was probably made by the firm of
T. Forester in the 1930s. They had been making
ceramics since the 19th century. Its bold and
stylish decoration would have complemented a
modern home in the 1930s.

138. STACKING SET

James Kent
1930s
Height 20.2 cms
Earthenware and transfer printed
Lent by Beverley

Known as the *Florita* pattern, this innovative and
wonderfully designed set comprising a teapot,
milk jug and cup, stack one on top of the other.
This kind of decoration is known as *Chintzware*
and was one of many fashionable and affordable
ranges, for everyday use, made in the '20s and
'30s. It is considered by some to be Art Deco,
although it is unlike any continental Art Deco. It
is quintessentially English, and has graced many a
British tea table.

139. VASE

Shelley
1931
Height 23.2 cms
Earthenware and hand-painted
Lent by Beverley

This vibrant design with its solid black
background has a pattern known as *Tulips*. It is a
standard Shelley shape, which was also used for
Harmony Ware, which has a *Dripware* glaze.

140. VASE

Radford for H.J. Wood
1930s
Height 11 cms
Earthenware and hand-painted
Lent by Beverley

Edward Radford (1882 - 1969) worked for
H.J. Wood on a freelance basis and designed
many similar and attractive pieces in the 1930s.
Many of these pieces were hand-painted in
pastel colours on a creamy coloured
background. These muted tones became
generally more popular with the British public as
the 1930s progressed.

141. MUG

Eric Ravilious for Wedgwood
1939
Height 11 cms
Earthenware and transfer printed
Lent by Manchester City Galleries

This mug by Eric Ravilious is decorated with the *Garden Implements* pattern and evolved from his previous *Garden* pattern. An extraordinary designer, Ravilious often used conventional shapes but his designs are unusual in their illustrative quality and subject matter.

142. JUG

A Susie Cooper Production for Crown Works
1930s
Height 13.1 cms
Earthenware and hand-painted
Lent by Nick Jones

This bold jug, decorated with a stylised floral
pattern, shows Susie Cooper's ability to breathe
new life into an everyday item. Simultaneously
cheerful and stylish, this jug would have been a
fun and functional piece of art for the home.

143. PLATE

A.E. Gray
Probably 1925
Diameter 24.6 cms
Bone china and hand-painted
The Nick Berthoud Collection

Part of the *Gloria Lustre* range, this brightly
coloured plate has a pattern possibly designed by
Susie Cooper. Gordon Forsyth was also involved
in the designs for *Gloria Lustre* and it is not
always possible to determine whether it was
Cooper or Forsyth who designed particular
pieces. We know, however, that the decorator of
this plate was Hilda May Lockett.

144. TEASET

Doulton
1930s
Height of teapot 12.6 cms
Earthenware and transfer printed
The John Clarke Collection

This part teaset is decorated with the *Caprice* pattern. It is a mixture of typical Art Deco styles; decorated with stylised flowers, and incorporating triangular handles and *Conical* shapes. Doulton made some very exciting tableware in the '30s and by the second half of the decade went on to produce simpler shapes and designs.

145. VASE

Frank Brangwyn for Royal Doulton
1930 - 1935
Height 30 cms
Earthenware and hand-painted
Lent by National Museums and Galleries of Wales

The painter and designer Frank Brangwyn (1867 - 1956), worked for William Morris designing tapestries in the 1890s. This pot has very stylised floral decoration in earthy colours and shows Brangwyn's interest in textiles. He designed tableware for Doulton and went on to design murals in England and America. He was knighted in 1941.

146. BISCUIT BARREL

Gray's Pottery
1930s
Height 13.7 cms
Earthenware and hand-painted
The Nick Berthoud Collection

The decoration on this biscuit barrel is created by loosely painted brushstrokes forming cheerful flowers and leaves. Biscuit barrels were very popular in the 1930s and were often used to serve biscuits with afternoon tea.

147. VASE

Wm. Moorcroft
1930s
Height 18 cms
Earthenware, tube lined and hand-painted
Lent by W. Moorcroft PLC, Burslem, Stoke-on-Trent

This is a conventionally shaped vase with a banded pattern based on and known as *Honesty*, a plant noted for its flattened silvery seedpods. This decorative motif was used in Art Nouveau interiors and can also be seen in the jewellery of the French designer Lalique. On this vase, made in the 1930s, the pattern has been given a more up-to-date twist.

ART DECO MEETS MODERNISM

There is an undefined meeting place between Art Deco and Modernism but theoretically they could not be more different.

Art Deco design looked to other cultures, art of the period, and historical design elements for inspiration. As well as form, pattern was an important part of its ethos. On the Continent it combines the handmade with the use of exotic and luxurious materials.

Modernist design was inspired by up and coming architects of the day and embraced the machine age, new technology, as well as the handmade. Pattern was much less important than form. Art Deco had no theory, whilst Modernism had a manifesto.

Ceramics was one of the places where Art Deco and Modernism met between the wars. If you look at the pieces by Keith Murray for Wedgwood, his training as an architect is easily detectable. His pots combine the handmade with new and old technology. The work by Greta Marks – trained at the Bauhaus in Germany – could be interpreted as either Modernist or Art Deco.

The Poole Pottery experimented with sumptuous glazes, as did Norman Wilson at Wedgwood. Both factories combined chemistry, new technology and the unpredictable effects of the kiln to produce stunning pots.

148. SUGAR BOWL AND MILK JUG
Carltonware
1930s
Height of sugar bowl 7 cms
Earthenware and hand-painted
National Museums Liverpool

This strikingly simple design, *Fin Rayure,* on the *Moderne* shape, is very European in influence. The French firm Robj produced a similar geometric cream coloured teaset trimmed with gold detailing in 1930. The balance and proportion of the design, as well as individual elements such as the elegantly waved handles, reappear in the pieces of the Carlton set seen here.

149. VASE

Shorter and Sons
1927 - 1932
Height 26 cms
Earthenware
Lent by Jill and Mike Newsham

This piece is quite different from those made previously by Shorter and Sons and it was probably designed by Clarice Cliff. She was known to subscribe to the French journal *Mobilier et Décoration* and to have taken some inspiration from designs shown there. Known as *Pyramus*, this vase has strong similarities in form to a vase by Robert Lallemant that was advertised in a 1929 edition of the journal. It has an unusual brilliant orange, uranium exterior glaze that contrasts with the blue glazed interior.

Interestingly, the names *Pyramus* and *Thisbe* are taken from Shakespeare's *A Midsummer Night's Dream* where they are two lovers in a play within a play. It is not known why the vases were marketed under these names, especially as the other names in the series are apparently unconnected.

150. VASE

Shorter and Sons
1927 - 1932
Height 25 cms
Earthenware
Lent by Jill and Mike Newsham

This *Thisbe* shape vase, probably designed by
Clarice Cliff, is one of a series of 5 produced; the
others are *Pyramus* (see above), *Rhomboid, Noni*
and *Olwen*. The *Thisbe* shape is very reminiscent
of the spiral form of the Great Minaret at
Samara, Iraq. The designer used simple,
architectural shapes and splendid glazes to
maximum effect. *Thisbe* has a *Turquoise Matt* glaze
that is often associated with this series. These
pieces were shown at the British Industries Fair
of 1930-31.

151. VASE
Susie Cooper Pottery
About 1936
Height 30.7 cms
Earthenware and incised
The Nick Berthoud Collection

With a matt glaze, this understated vase has decoration carved into the
body, and is known as *Incised Ware*. Susie Cooper is distinguished from many
other ceramic designers of the 1930s because of her diversity of techniques.
She gave the British public what they wanted, but she was not afraid to try
new and innovative designs, or in this case use an older form of decoration.

152. COFFEE CAN AND SAUCER
A Susie Cooper Production for Crown Works
1930s
Can height 5.8 cms
Earthenware
National Museums Liverpool

Traditional in shape, this coffee can and saucer is
playfully decorated with simple marks incised
through the red enamel. Susie Cooper is
demonstrating how a simple and economical
pattern can still look very striking.

153. JUG

Unmarked
1930s
Height 7 cms
Earthenware and hand-painted
The Nick Berthoud Collection

This jug is part of a range of hand-thrown and
decorated wares designed by Susie Cooper and dates
from about 1933. They are sometimes described today
as *Studio Wares* because of their hand crafting.

154. TEAPOT

Greta Marks for Greta Pottery
1937 - 1940
Height 15 cms
Earthenware and hand-painted
Lent by the Potteries Museum & Art Gallery, Stoke-on-Trent

155. BOWL

Greta Marks for Ridgways
1937 - 1939
Height 17.2 cms
Earthenware
Lent by the Potteries Museum & Art Gallery, Stoke-on-Trent

These pieces are designed by Greta Marks (1899 - 1990), who was a former student at the Bauhaus School in Weimar, Germany – a radical art school which sought to combine the principles of the machine age with the hand-crafted. Greta and her husband subsequently opened a factory in Germany producing a range of domestic tableware influenced by Greta's training at the Bauhaus. The tableware was sold in England in Ambrose Heal's store in London. By 1935 her husband had died and the Nazi regime in Germany had made life difficult for her and her two sons and so she fled to England. After teaching at the Central School of Art in Burslem she went on to work for Minton.

Greta then went on to establish her own firm, Greta Pottery, producing simply decorated pieces on *Biscuit Ware* bought in from many firms, and designing shapes and patterns with E. Brain and Co., and Ridgways. She met and married Harold Marks in 1938, and in 1945 they moved to London where she painted and made pottery.

156. DISH
John Adams for Poole Pottery
1930s
Width 22 cms
Earthenware
The John Clarke Collection

This dish is part of a very striking series known as
Plane Ware. Also produced in other colours it has
wing-like attachments on either side. Modernist in
design it would also have sat comfortably in an
Art Deco interior of the 1930s.

157. VASE
John Adams for Poole Pottery
1920s
Height 36 cms
Earthenware
The John Clarke Collection

Known as *Chinese Blue*, this glaze, applied over a
red earthenware pot, was designed and
developed by John Adams in the 1920s. This type
of ware is sometimes dependant on the
unpredictable effects of the kiln. It would have sat
comfortably in either a Traditional or a Modernist
interior of the period.

158. VASE
John Adams for Poole Pottery
1930s
Height 17.5 cms
Earthenware
The John Clarke Collection

Not everything produced at the Poole Pottery in
the 1920s and '30s was highly decorated. John
Adams issued some wonderful Modernist shapes
with fine glazes between 1930-33. This piece of
Everest Ware, with its banded decoration, is
reminiscent of what Keith Murray was producing
at Wedgwood at the time.

159. PLANT-POT
Poole Pottery
Late 1930s
Height 22 cms
Earthenware
The John Clarke Collection

Known as Sylvan *Ware*, this plant-pot was especially
produced to be used on the luxury liner the *Queen Mary*,
built at the John Brown Shipyard on the Clyde in 1936. They
were also sold through the Liverpool shop R. Reynolds and
Son Ltd in Canning Place.

160. VASE

Keith Murray for Wedgwood
About 1935
Height 20 cms
Basalt
Lent by the Trustees of the Wedgwood Museum

Keith Murray combined old techniques with new Modernist values in creating this piece. Hand-thrown, this vase is made from basalt – a stoneware first produced in black by Josiah Wedgwood in the 1760s. Norman Wilson pioneered the bronze basalt body (formerly known as copper basalt) in the 1930s. This coloured vase was only produced for a limited period. It has a form of banded decoration known as engine-turning, also first used by Wedgwood in the 1760s. The shapes of pots designed by the French designer Jean Luce possibly further inspired Murray. These were illustrated in the Decorative Art Studio Year Book of 1932.

161. COFFEE POT

Keith Murray for Wedgwood
About 1932
Height 20.2 cms
Earthenware
Lent by the Trustees of the Wedgwood Museum

This coffee pot shape was designed by Keith Murray and is part of a set. Its stylish shape is enhanced by the banding of *Platinum Lustre*. The *Moonstone* glaze is by Norman Wilson.

162. VASE
Keith Murray for Wedgwood
About 1935
Height 19 cms
Earthenware
Lent by the Trustees of the Wedgwood Museum

This is one of the more common pieces connected with the designer Keith Murray. It is hand thrown and has a lovely *Matt Green* glaze. This is a colour closely associated with home interiors of the 1930s. Wedgwood, at a time of financial instability, found it more economical to have pots hand thrown, rather then spend money on costly moulds. If a line did not sell well then little money was lost.

By 1935 Keith Murray's work was renowned and in the same year his pots formed part of an important exhibition held at the Royal Academy and attracted much attention.

163. VASE
Keith Murray for Wedgwood
1930s
Height 39 cms
Earthenware
Lent by B. Meyer

This understated vase with its beautiful blue glaze is by one of the finest Modernist designers, Keith Murray. Murray began working for Wedgwood in 1932 and went on to design numerous pieces of tableware. He demonstrates his training as an architect with his elegant use of simple sculptural forms. Possibly made as a prototype, this vase is very rare.

164. BOWL

Keith Murray for Wedgwood
1930s
Diameter 17 cms
Earthenware
Lent by B. Meyer

Keith Murray designed many functional pieces for
Wedgwood using new ceramic bodies and glazes.
Because of the simplicity and purity of Murray's
designs, they remained fashionable, with some
pieces being produced throughout the Second
World War. Using his architectural skills, Murray
designed the new Wedgwood factory at Barlaston,
which opened in 1940.

165. CADBURY BOURNVITA POT

Wedgwood
About 1934
Height 20.5 cms
Earthenware
Lent by the Trustees of the Wedgwood Museum

Cadbury's Bournvita was first produced from
1933. The designer of this *Honey Buff* coloured
pot, which was specifically made for the malted
chocolate drink, is unknown. During its history
Bournvita has been marketed as an aid to vitality
and energy, and also as a relaxing bedtime
beverage. The Bournvita sets were so popular
during the period that at one time their
production provided work for over 200 people.

166. VASE
Norman Wilson for Wedgwood
1930s
Height 21 cms
Earthenware
Lent by the Trustees of the Wedgwood Museum

This *Queen's Ware* vase is part of Norman
Wilson's (1902 - 1988) *Unique* range. He was
interested in the simplicity of the shapes of
Chinese and Korean ceramics, and used these to
create new forms. Wilson used two different
coloured glazes to highlight the shape in a
Modernist style. He was an imaginative
researcher and experimenter involved in the
development of many successful glazes, such as
Matt Straw, in the 1930s.

167. DISH

Norman Wilson for Wedgwood
1930s
Height 9 cms
Earthenware
Lent by the Trustees of the Wedgwood Museum

This dish is part of Norman Wilson's *Unique* range. It has a *Mottled Blue and Green* glaze which is enhanced by the fluting. Norman Wilson, after leaving the North Staffordshire Technical College, worked for his father, who was a china manufacturer, before emigrating to Canada to break in polo ponies. Encouraged by Frank Wedgwood he returned to England and was appointed as Works Manager at Etruria in 1927.

168. DISH

Norman Wilson for Wedgwood
1930s
Height 7.6 cms
Earthenware
Lent by the Trustees of the Wedgwood Museum

The *Aventurine* glaze, on this dish from the *Unique* range, contains the mineral haematite, sometimes known as 'Fools Gold'. This gives it a shimmering and sparkly quality. Pots like this, although not obviously Art Deco in style, are part of an experimental phase in British ceramics in the 1920s and '30s and they would have sat comfortably in an Art Deco or Modernist interior of the period.

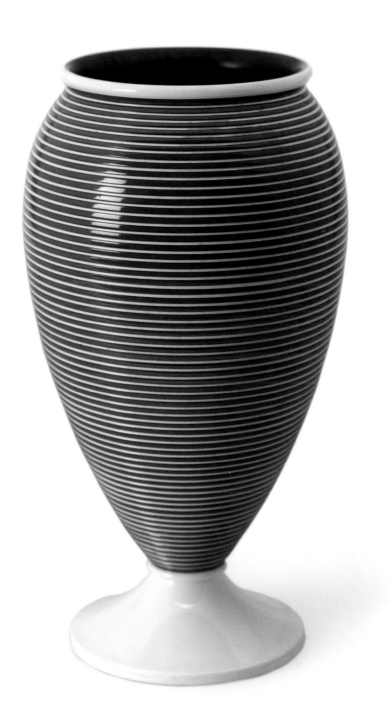

169. VASE

Norman Wilson for Wedgwood
1930s
Height 27.8 cms
Earthenware
Lent by the Trustees of the Wedgwood Museum

This ribbed vase is a fine example of Norman Wilson's skill. Not only a master potter and inventor, he introduced the first gas-fired tunnel ovens at the factory. His versatility and inventiveness contributed to Wedgwood's modernisation and success during the Depression era.

170. VASE
Shelley
1930s
Height 15cms
Earthenware
Lent by Beverley

171. PLATE
Shelley
1930s
Diameter 35.5 cms
Earthenware
Lent by Muir Hewitt

Although the decoration on these pieces from the *Harmony* range appears to be random, it actually requires a reasonable amount of skill to create the desired effect. Eric Slater discovered the *Dripware* technique by accident whilst experimenting on a potter's wheel with coloured glazes and paint thinners such as turpentine. He realised that there were extensive commercial possibilities, exhibiting the range at the 1933 British Industries Fair and producing a wide range of Harmony decorated goods for sale.

172. VASE
Clarice Cliff for Newport Pottery
1935
Height 19.4 cms
Earthenware and hand-painted
The John Clarke Collection

This vase is part of a series known as *Milano*. The range includes various shapes usually decorated in black and one other colour. It appears more Modernist in shape than Art Deco and is an unusual piece from Clarice Cliff.

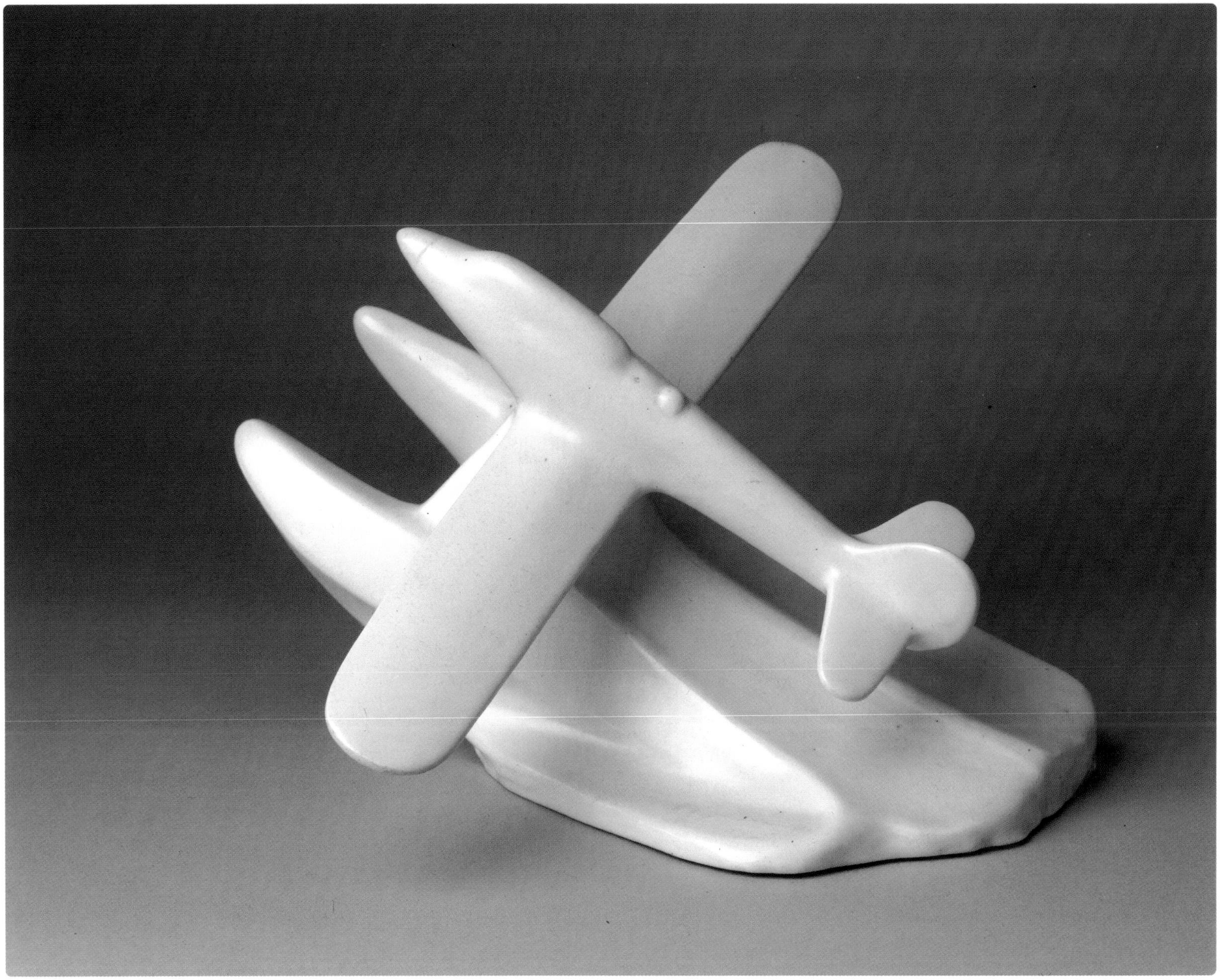

173. FIGURE
Unmarked
Late 1920s
Height 20.5 cms
Earthenware
Lent by the Potteries Museum & Art Gallery, Stoke-on-Trent

This simply modelled and glazed aeroplane is based on the Supermarine S4 plane designed by R.J. Mitchell in 1925 that was entered for the Schneider Trophy. The trophy was devised by Jacques Schneider, a former air and balloon pilot who, because of a serious accident, was no longer able to fly. He realised in 1912 that seaplane design was lagging behind other aircraft. He considered that seaplanes would be the best solution to long-range passenger service. So on the 5 December 1912 he offered a trophy for a seaplane race over at least 150 nautical miles. This he believed would be the best away to encourage designers to build more advanced planes. The S4 was a very advanced cantilever monoplane that had already set a world speed record. However, on the test run for the trophy the plane crashed, but fortunately the pilot's life was saved. The designer and maker of the model shown here is unknown.

174. TEAPOT

A. Wood
1921 - 1925
Height 9.5 cms
Earthenware
The Nick Berthoud Collection

Cube teapots were created by a number of companies under
licence. It seems that this example is made by Wood and
Sons, but the shape has then been decorated by a different
company: A.E. Gray & Co. The *Yellow Lustre* decoration simply
sets off the modern shape. The *Cube* teapot was a remarkable
invention; as Cube Teapots Ltd. claimed in their 1925 advert
that it was 'the brilliant climax in teapot construction'. The
progressive design was made to minimise troublesome drips
from the spout, the lid locked on securely, and the square
shape enabled caterers to stack and store teapots safely with
the most efficient use of the space available. The convenience
and compactness of the pot led to the adoption of *Cube* tea
services by the Cunard Line in the late 1920s.